AL STEVENS
TEACHES C

An Interactive Tutorial

AL STEVENS

M&T BOOKS

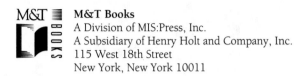

M&T Books
A Division of MIS:Press, Inc.
A Subsidiary of Henry Holt and Company, Inc.
115 West 18th Street
New York, New York 10011

97   96   95   94   4   3   2   1

Development Editor: Debra Williams Cauley
Copy and Technical Editor: Betsy Hardinger
Production Editor: Patricia Wallenburg

Dedication

To Bernie, Jennifer, and Cathy Stevens, three ladies
of considerable grace and stature whose strength and courage
carried us all through a time of deep personal loss.

Acknowledgments

Thanks are due to Bob Brodt, a fine programmer whose shareware Small C Interpreter inspired the original Quincy program. His influence on Quincy's architecture has persisted throughout all the versions over the years.

This project would not have been possible without the support and encouragement of Jon Erickson, the managing editor of *Dr. Dobb's Journal*.

Special thanks go to Judy Stevens, my wife and best friend, who spent countless hours validating the exercises and testing each new version of Quincy.

Table of Contents

Chapter 3

Functions 55

Chapter 6
Library Functions 151

Appendix

PREFACE

*W*hy another book about C? Good question. There are dozens of excellent books that describe C to the programmer, most of them written by acknowledged experts in the field. What sets this book apart? What contributed to my decision to undertake this project?

First, *Al Stevens Teaches C* fills a gap among the introductory programming texts that I have written. *Welcome to Programming*, published in 1994 by MIS:Press, introduces the world of software development to the computer-literate user who wants to learn how to write programs. *Teach Yourself C++*, now in its third edition and also from MIS:Press, is a tutorial book for C programmers who want to learn C++. This book fits nicely between those two. It teaches C to the student who already understands programming.

The second reason for writing this book comes from my experience teaching C and lecturing about it to programmers and educators. Students need an introductory text that walks them through the language in a sequence that starts at the beginning and builds each lesson on the ones that precede it. Instructors need a book with clear explanations, just enough but not too much detail at any given level, and well-thought-out topics and exercises. This book reflects my opinions about how such a C tutorial should be structured.

A third reason comes from my six years as author of the C Programming Column in *Dr. Dobb's Journal*, the top-rated monthly magazine for programmers. In that time I have published more than 100,000 lines of C code and have read a lot of code written by other programmers. My views about what constitutes good code have been shaped by that experience, and I believe that a student learns good or bad programming habits from the outset. A good tutorial sets a good example with code that demonstrates not only the object lesson at hand but also sound and reliable code. The examples in this book strive to reach that goal.

Finally, I believe that students learn a programming language more quickly when the language tool they use is well integrated with the lessons. Rather than using a commercial compiler product to load, compile, and run the exercises, the student who reads *Al Stevens Teaches C* uses *Quincy*, a C interpreter included on the companion diskette. Quincy is a Standard C interpreter with a tutorial mode that follows the exercises in the book, loading the correct source code file for each one and keeping track of the student's progress.

This book strives to meet all those goals: providing an organized, structured approach to a C language tutorial; teaching good programming by setting good examples; and using a C language development system that is closely integrated with the tutorial exercises.

Al Stevens

1994

Chapter 1

An Introduction to Programming in C

The C programming language is approximately 20 years old. In that time C has evolved from a small tool that a programmer in a research laboratory built for himself and some colleagues into the worldwide language of choice for two generations of programmers. C boasts an international published standard definition, compilers for virtually every computer and operating system, and the distinction of being the language with which most contemporary applications, operating systems, and software tools are written.

Who Are You?

To read and understand this book, you should have some background in computer programming. You do not necessarily need to be a seasoned programmer, but you should know what programming is and how programmers write code that compilers compile and computers execute. You should understand typical programming issues such as arithmetic and relational operators in expressions, operator precedence, data types, constants, and input/output. You should be familiar with the different base notations—decimal, octal, hexadecimal, and binary—for representing numbers in a computer. Anyone with a knowledge of BASIC, FORTRAN, COBOL, Pascal, or any structured, procedural programming language will have no trouble following the lessons in this book. Assembly language programmers take immediately to C because it offers the same low-level access to the hardware but with the notation of a structured high-level language.

If you do not have such a programming background, you can begin with my earlier book *Welcome to Programming*, published by MIS:Press. It uses the QBasic language to teach the fundamentals of programming. A student can move readily from that book to this one to learn C programming.

This book also serves the advanced, experienced programmer who just wants to learn the syntax and grammar of C. It contains concise descriptions of each topic with short exercise programs that demonstrate the lesson being learned.

What Do You Need?

The companion diskette (in a pocket on the inside back cover) and an IBM PC-compatible computer running MS-DOS are all that you need. The diskette contains the source code for the exercises. Unlike most C books, which require the reader to provide a C compiler, this one includes *Quincy*, a C language interpreter that you can use to run all the exercises as well as write your own C programs. Quincy is a small system, consisting of one executable program, some standard library source header files, an on-line help database, and a tutorial help database. Quincy's tutorial mode goes hand-in-hand with the tutorial exercises in the book. As you read the book, you can load the exercises, run them, change them, and see how the C language behaves. The tutorial keeps track of your progress and always starts up where you left off. In addition to the exercises, the companion diskette has several other example programs that you can run with Quincy to learn more about the kinds of programs that you can develop in C.

Eventually you will learn all that this book can teach, and you will want to write C programs that are larger and more complex than Quincy can support. For that you need one of the many C compiler products that are available for the PC, the Macintosh, the PowerPC, the Atari, the Amiga, or whichever computer you are going to write programs for.

A Brief History of C

In the early 1970s, Dennis Ritchie, a programmer at AT&T Bell Laboratories in Murray Hill, New Jersey, adapted *B*—a *typeless* programming language with structures similar to those in ALGOL—into the first version of what he named C. Ritchie's goal was to provide a language that would allow the programmer to access the hardware much like assembly language did, but with structured programming constructs similar to those found in high-level languages. He included integer and pointer data types that mapped directly over the hardware registers of the PDP-11 minicomputer, and he took advantage of the PDP-11's hardware stack architecture to support recursive functions.

C, as originally designed, ran on the AT&T in-house UNIX multiuser, multitasking operating system, which ran first on the PDP-7 and then on the PDP-11. When Ritchie rewrote the UNIX C compiler in C itself, and when UNIX developer Ken Thompson successfully rewrote UNIX in C, they made programming history. UNIX became the first major operating system to be written in something other than assembly language. When they ported the C compiler to other computers, the developers turned UNIX into the first operating system able to run on many different platforms, a truly portable operating system. Porting UNIX became a matter of porting the C compiler, recoding some very few assembly language low-level driver programs, and recompiling the operating system itself. These achievements distinguished C as a unique language, one that could be used to write systems programs—previously the exclusive domain of assembly language—and one that could be used to write portable programs, a goal never achieved by the high-level languages that came before it.

For years, C existed mainly in UNIX systems, and UNIX remained an internal AT&T operating system. Eventually, AT&T made UNIX available to universities at virtually no cost, and a generation of students was exposed to it and to C. Those students left school and entered the field of programming with experience in and a love for UNIX and C. This influence eventually found its way into corporate America, and C began to enjoy mainstream support in circles previously dominated by COBOL at the top and assembly language at the bottom.

Although C's origins are in the research labs of big business and academia, its widespread acceptance outside those walls was assured when developers provided C compilers for the first personal computers. Early microcomputers ran on the 8080 and Z80 microprocessors under the CP/M operating system. At first, BASIC was the dominant programming language, with assembly language running a close second. Eventually, however, vendors published C compilers for those computers, and programmers of the so-called home computers began making the switch. The IBM PC, introduced in 1981, and the clones that followed continued this trend. C rapidly became the programmers' favorite language for writing programs under MS-DOS. At one time more than a dozen C compilers were available for the PC. Most of the applications and systems software for the PC are written in C or its object-oriented extension, C++. MS-DOS itself consists of C programs, as do most of its utility programs. The Windows graphical operating environment is written in C. Even Windows NT, the newest Microsoft operating system, is written mostly in C.

C was originally defined in 1981 in *The C Programming Language* by Brian Kernighan and Dennis Ritchie, published by Prentice Hall. The book was not a formal language specification, but it described C the way Ritchie had implemented it. The book became known simply as K&R, for the initials of its authors, and the dialect of C that it described was, for many years, called K&R C. Some programmers have renamed K&R C *Classic C*. Over the years, the compiler builders added features to C according to the requirements of its users. As the industry accepted those extensions, a newer dialect came into being and a *de facto* standard evolved.

In 1983, the American National Standards Institute (ANSI) formed a committee whose task it was to define a standard definition of the C language based on the industry's *de facto* standard. They were joined by a committee of the International Standards Organization (ISO), which formed to define the language for the international programming community. The combined committees published a standard document in 1990. The language that they defined is known as *Standard C*. A second edition of the K&R book describes Standard C, obscuring somewhat the identity of K&R C. This book teaches Standard C.

C's Continuing Role

You might wonder about C's future given the current popularity of C++ and object-oriented programming. Will C++ displace C as the language of choice? Most likely it will. Does that spell the demise of C as a viable programming language? Definitely not. Few good programming languages are completely killed off. There are almost always development circumstances where they excel, and usually there are existing programs to maintain.

In the first place, C++ is a superset of C. You need to know C in order to program in C++. Furthermore, C is more suitable than C++ for solving some programming problems. Many staunch C++ advocates do not always acknowledge this position, but it is true, nonetheless. Contemporary C++ software development environments are big. They use lots of disk space and require advanced computers with megabytes of extended memory. These requirements grow with each new version of the language and each new release of the compilers. Most C++ compilers are oriented toward graphical user interface environments such as Windows and OS/2 Presentation Manager. They are not particularly well suited for developing small programs to run on small systems. Object-oriented programs that use complex class hierarchies tend to be huge programs that do not run as efficiently as their C language procedural counterparts. C, which is a traditional procedural programming language, is a better choice for writing device drivers, utility programs, embedded applications, and most text processing applications.

Having learned C, do you need to move on to C++? It would not be a bad idea. Most programming opportunities in the next several years will involve C++ class libraries that encapsulate the application program interfaces (APIs) of Windows, the PowerPC, OS/2, and others. Before you learn C++, however, you must learn C. Most C++ introductory books assume that the student already knows C, and this book fills that need. When you have finished this book, you can move on to my book, *Teach Yourself C++*, published by MIS:Press.

A Brief Description of C

In Chapter 2, you begin to write C programs. This introduction describes C at the elementary level. You will learn more about each of these concepts by using the exercises in the chapters that follow. As you proceed through the lessons, return to this synopsis and see how what it says begins to fall into place.

C is a *procedural* programming language, which means that you design and code programs as procedural modules. The procedural modules in a C program are called *functions*. Every C program begins execution in a function named *main* and terminates when the main function returns.

The main function calls lower-level functions, which in turn call lower-level functions. A function starts execution at its first, topmost statement and continues until the last, bottom-most statement executes or until the function executes a *return* statement from somewhere inside the function body. Each function, upon completion, returns to its caller. Execution then continues with the next program statement.

You read a C program from the top to the bottom, but the functions do not have to be coded in that sequence. However, all declarations of functions and variables must be coded in the program above any statements that reference them. You can declare a function by simply writing it or by providing a *function prototype* that describes its name, return value, and parameters to the compiler. If you provide a function prototype ahead of any calls to the function, you can put the function itself anywhere in the program. The function's declaration and all calls to it must match the prototype with respect to its return type and the types of its parameters.

Functions may contain *parameters*. The caller of the function passes *arguments* that the function uses as its parameters. The argument types must match the types of the parameters declared for the function.

Some functions return a value and others do not. The caller of a function that returns a value can code the function call on the right side of an *assignment* statement, assigning the returned value to a named data variable. You can also code a function call as the argument that provides the parameter to another function call, as an *initializer* to a local data variable, or as a member of an *expression*.

Each function consists of one or more *blocks* of statements. The blocks are nested. Each block can have its own local variables, which remain in scope as long as statements at or below that block level are executing. A C program can also have variables declared outside any function. Those variables are said to have *global* scope because the statements in all the functions in the same source file can reference them.

Statements are one of the following: declarations, which declare *variables* and functions; definitions, which define instances of variables and functions; or procedural statements, which are executable code statements that reside inside a function's definition.

A variable *declaration* specifies the variable's storage class, data type, type qualifier, level of indirection (if it is a pointer), name, and dimensions (if it is an array). A function declaration is more frequently called its prototype and declares the function's return type, name, and the number and types of its arguments.

A variable *definition* includes the components of a declaration and may include an initializer if the variable has an initializing value. A definition defines the instance of the variable and reserves memory for it. A function definition contains the function's executable code.

Usually, a variable's declaration and definition are the same statement. A function's prototype and definition are usually in different places.

Procedural statements are either assignments, expressions, or *program flow control* statements. An expression is a program statement that returns a value. An expression can stand on its own or be on the right side of an assignment statement. Expressions consist of variables, constants, operators, and function calls.

C uses the control structures of structured programming, which include *sequence* (one statement executing after another), *iteration* (*for* and *while* loops), and *selection* (*if-then-else* and *switch-case* control structures). C also permits unstructured programming with the *goto* statement.

Unlike other languages such as COBOL, BASIC, and FORTRAN, C has no built-in input/output statements. Instead, input and output are implemented by C functions found in one of several standard libraries. Many language features that are built into other languages are performed instead by functions in C. Data conversions, string manipulations, output formatting, memory allocation, and many other operations are performed by functions taken from function libraries. C itself is a small language capable only of declaring variables, assigning expressions to variables, and calling functions—only one of which, *main*, is actually defined as a part of the language proper. C's power comes in the way that it is extended with functions. In the early days, the function libraries and their implementation were left largely to the individual compiler vendors. Today, a large part of ANSI Standard C is the definition of a standard set of functions in a standard suite of function libraries that perform in defined ways.

The Organization of This Book

Each chapter in this book teaches a subject of the C language. The chapters follow a tutorial progression. I assume in each chapter that you have completed the chapters that precede it.

The exercises consist of brief, complete programs that you can run with Quincy or that you can compile with a C compiler and run from the DOS command line. Each exercise has a file name that identifies the chapter and exercise number. For example, the file named EX02003.C would be Exercise 3 in Chapter 2.

From time to time I briefly describe the behavior of some aspect of C and then ask you to take it on faith until later. Do not let these apparent leaps discourage you. Sometimes I must use a part of the language that you have not yet learned so that I can demonstrate the part that you are learning now. Be patient. I use that approach only when I cannot avoid it. Eventually everything makes sense.

Chapter 2 is where you begin writing programs. I teach you about the *main* function, how to put comments in your code, how to include the header files of the standard library functions, and how to perform simple console output to view the results of your programs. You learn about C expressions and assignment statements. You learn how to read data from the keyboard and display information on the screen.

Chapter 3 is about functions. I show you how C programs define and call functions, passing parameter arguments and getting return values. You learn how C functions are arranged into nested blocks of code.

Chapter 4 is about program flow control. You learn the *if...else*, *do*, *while*, *for*, *goto*, *switch*, and *return* operators. You learn how to use *setjmp* and *longjmp* to return from a point deep in the nested functions of a program to a defined place at a higher level. You learn how to use recursive functions in a C program.

In Chapter 5 I teach the C data types, including characters, integers, and floating point numbers. You learn how to use constants and pointers in your programs. You learn about the scope of variables. You see how to arrange data types into aggregates called *arrays*, *structures*, and *unions* and how to define new data type identifiers with the *typedef* operator.

Chapter 6 identifies the Standard C library functions that Quincy supports. You learn how to use header files for the standard functions that your programs call. You learn about string functions, memory allocation functions, math functions, and others.

Chapter 7 is about file input/output. You learn how to use the functions in **stdio.h** to read and write the console and print reports, and create, read, write, modify, and delete disk files.

Chapter 8 is about the C *preprocessor*, which allows you to define macros and write compile-time conditional expressions that control how a program compiles.

Chapter 9 contains several small case studies—example programs to give you an idea of the kinds of programs that you might write. You learn how to write filter programs that use MS-DOS or UNIX input/output redirection to pipe data between programs.

The Appendix is the Quincy C Interpreter User's Guide.

The glossary defines some common C programming terms. If I use a term in the book that you do not know, look it up in the glossary.

Chapter 2

WRITING SIMPLE C PROGRAMS

*T*his chapter is your starting point for learning C. We jump that first hurdle—writing the first program. Then I introduce the data components of a C program: variables and constants. Use the exercises in this chapter to learn these basic lessons:

▼ Writing the *main* function
▼ The **stdio.h** library header file
▼ Comments
▼ Data types
▼ Assignments and expressions
▼ Console input and output

Your First Program

C programs consist of variables and functions. A function consists of statements. Every C program begins with a function named *main*. The best way to get started is with a real program. Exercise 2.1 is your first C program, one that has a *main* function and several other fundamental C language constructs.

EXERCISE 2.1 *Your first C program.*

```
/* ----- ex02001.c ----- */
#include <stdio.h>

main()
{
    puts("My first C program"); /* write to the screen */
}
```

This is a good time to turn to the Appendix and learn how to use Quincy to step through the tutorial exercises and run the programs shown in the book.

N O T E

Exercise 2.1 is a small program that illustrates a lot of what a C programmer uses. It has some source code comments, includes a standard library header file, declares a *main* function, and writes a message on the screen.

Comments

The first line of code in Exercise 2.1 is a program *comment*. Comments in a program's source code document the meaning of the code. They have no effect on the executable program itself.

C comments begin with the /* character sequence and continue through the */ character sequence. Comments may span several source code lines and may not be nested. They may occupy lines of their own, or they may coexist on lines that have other code. For example, the next to the last line in Exercise 2.1 has both an executable statement and a comment.

Use comments throughout your programs. Make them meaningful with respect to what they convey to programmers who might be reading your code. Do not make the two common mistakes that many programmers make: (1) assuming that you will be the only programmer who reads your code and (2) assuming that you will always remember why you wrote a program a certain way. Comments document your intentions. Use them. The exercises and example programs in this book use comments liberally.

N O T E

By convention, the first line of code in each of this book's programs is a comment that names the source code file. You see these comments on the screen when you load the exercise programs into Quincy or your programmer's editor or integrated development environment, but beyond Exercise 2.1, I do not show them; the captions identify the programs.

#include

The second line of code in Exercise 2.1 is the *#include <stdio.h>* statement. This statement is a *preprocessing directive*. We'll discuss the preprocessor in Chapter 8. The *#include* directive tells the compiler to include a different source code file in the program. Exercise 2.1 includes the file named **stdio.h**, a standard library header file that describes functions and global values used for console and file input and output. The exercise includes the header file so that it can call the *puts* (pronounced *put-ess*) function. Most exercises in this book include **stdio.h**, which is why I mention it here. Do not worry too much about what is in the header file just yet. It becomes clear soon enough.

The file name in the *#include* directive is enclosed by *angle brackets*, which is another name for the combined use of the less-than and greater-than symbols. This usage identifies header files that the compiler system supplies. When you include your own header files, you surround those names with double quotes. Chapter 8 has more details about this feature.

White Space

The third line in Exercise 2.1 is a blank line. The C language is a free-form language, which means that white space characters—spaces, tabs, and blank lines—are extra. Except for the rare occasion where two keywords or identifiers are separated by a space (such as *else if*), a program needs no white space at all to compile. (An exception is the white space inside string constants, which I describe later.) Without white space, however, the program would be unreadable by people. Programmers use white space to indent and separate code in various styles.

There are many styles for writing C code. I take no position with regard to style, although the exercises do reflect my preferences. You see other styles in the programs of other people who use different conventions for indenting and the placement of brace characters. There is no one right way. Choose a style that works for you. Try, however, to make it legible, and be consistent in its use.

Identifiers

A C program consists of variables and functions, all of which have names. The name of a function or variable is called its *identifier*. As the programmer, you assign identifiers to the parts of your program. Following are the rules for identifiers in the C language.

▼ An identifier consists of letters, digits, and the underscore character.

▼ An identifier must begin with a letter. (Underscores are allowed in the first character, but, by convention, leading underscores are reserved for identifiers that the compiler defines.)

▼ Identifiers are case-sensitive. For example, *MyFunc* and *myfunc* are different identifiers.

▼ An identifier may be any length, but only the first 32 characters are significant. Some C implementations restrict the significance of external identifiers (ones with global scope) to six characters. This is because of limitations in the particular linker program and not because of any limitation in the C language.

▼ An identifier may not be one of the reserved C keywords, listed next.

Keywords

Table 2.1 lists the keywords that are reserved by the C language. You must not use any of these keywords as identifiers in your program. I'll show you how to use each of them as the chapters and exercises progress.

TABLE 2.1 *C Keywords.*

auto	break	case	char
const	continue	default	do
double	else	enum	extern
float	for	goto	if
int	long	register	return
short	signed	sizeof	static
struct	switch	typedef	union
unsigned	void	volatile	while

The *main* Function

The fourth line in Exercise 2.1 declares and defines the *main* function. Every C program has a function named *main*. It contains the entry and exit points of the program. The program begins executing with the first statement in *main* and terminates when the *main* function returns.

The *main* function in the exercise illustrates several things about C functions in general. The first line provides the function's name. Other functions in a program have other names. The only required function name is *main*. After that, you are free to name functions anything you want as long as you stay within the rules given above for naming identifiers.

The parentheses after the function's name contain the function's *parameter list*. In this case, *main* has no parameters, so the parameter list is empty. An empty parameter list is represented by the ( ) character sequence.

The *function body* follows the parameter list. The function body begins with a left brace character ({) and ends with a right brace character (}). In between are the function's statements, the lines of code that execute when the function is called. Exercise 2.1 has only one statement.

Statements are terminated with a semicolon.

A brace-surrounded group of statements is called a *statement block*. Statement blocks may be nested. You see how this nesting contributes to program control flow in Chapter 4. Exercise 2.1 has only one statement block.

A function is finished executing after its last statement executes or when the *return* statement executes. Exercise 2.1 allows the *main* function to terminate by reaching the end of the outermost—in this case, the only—statement block, which contains only one statement.

Console Output

The single executable statement in Exercise 2.1's function body is a *function call* to the standard library function *puts*. The *puts* function writes a string of character data on the system console, which is the video screen on a PC. The string to be written is specified in the *string constant* argument between the parentheses that follow the function name. The statement passes the address of the string constant to the *puts* function. What happens next depends on what the *puts* function does. Just as a BASIC programmer knows that the PRINT statement writes data to the screen, a C programmer knows that the standard *puts* function does somewhat the same thing. The important difference is that PRINT is part of the BASIC language—a built-in operator—while *puts* happens to be the name that some programmer many years ago gave to the standard library function that displays a string on the screen. It could just as easily been any other name, and there are other functions that do screen output.

Variables

You saw in Exercise 2.1 how a C program declares a function. Programs declare data variables, too, each of which has a *type*. The type defines the format and behavior of the variable. C supports character, integer, and floating point data types. C has four basic built-in data types, called the *intrinsic* data types. They are: *char*, *int*, *float*, and *double*. You can define data records with the *struct* and *union* types.

Each variable declaration in a program provides its type and identifier. Variables can have other properties as well. Type specifiers can include *unsigned*, *long*, or *short* to further define the type. You can use the *static*, *extern*, *register*, and *auto* storage classes. There are *const* and *volatile* type qualifiers. I teach these things in this and later chapters.

The size of a variable depends on its type. The size of each type depends on the C implementation. The examples in this book use data types with sizes typical of C compilers for the PC.

Next, you will learn to declare variables of each of the types. Later you will learn how to put those declarations into their proper context in a program.

Characters

A *char* variable contains one character from the computer's character set. Characters in PC implementations of the C language are contained in eight-bit bytes using the ASCII character set to represent character values. A program declares a character variable with the *char* type specification as shown here.

```
char ch;
```

The declaration just shown declares a variable of type *char* with the identifier *ch*. Once you declare a variable in this manner, the program can reference it in expressions, which are discussed in the next section.

Exercise 2.2 illustrates the use of the *char* variable.

EXERCISE 2.2 *Using the char variable.*

```
#include <stdio.h>
main()
{
    char c;        /* char variable  */
    c = 'b';       /* assign 'b' to c */
    putchar(c);    /* display 'b'     */
    c = 'y';       /* assign 'y' to c */
    putchar(c);    /* display 'y'     */
    c = 'e';       /* assign 'e' to c */
    putchar(c);    /* display 'e'     */
}
```

Exercise 2.2 uses the standard *putchar* function, which displays a single character, to display this message on the screen:

```
bye
```

Exercise 2.2 also introduces the assignment statement, which I address in more detail later in this chapter. An assignment assigns a value to a variable. The value can be a complex expression, but until you get to that point, the exercises use simple constants. The 'b', 'y', and 'e' values are ASCII character constant expressions in the C language.

> **N O T E**   If you are guessing that there must be a better way to display the "bye" message, you are right. At the very least you could use the *puts* function and a "bye" string constant similar to what Exercise 2.1 did. Exercise 2.2, however, contrives to show you how the *char* data type is declared and used.

You can declare an *unsigned char* variable this way:

```
unsigned char c;
```

Unless they are *unsigned*, *char* variables behave like eight-bit signed quantities when you use them in arithmetic and comparison operations. Some compilers allow *char* variables to default to the *unsigned* property as an option, but this behavior is nonstandard C. Normally, you must include the *unsigned* specification to get unsigned behavior.

Integers

Variables of integer types come in several varieties. The basic integer is a signed quantity, and you declare one with the *int* type specifier like this:

```
int Counter;
```

An integer can be *unsigned*, *long*, *short*, or just a plain signed integer like the one just shown. Here are some declarations that show some of the different kinds of integers:

```
long int Amount;        /* a long integer             */
long Quantity;          /* a long integer             */
unsigned int Offset;    /* an unsigned integer        */
unsigned Offset;        /* an unsigned integer        */
short SmallAmt;         /* a short integer            */
unsigned short Lester;  /* an unsigned short integer  */
unsigned short int Landon; /* an unsigned short integer  */
```

As the examples show, you can omit the *int* keyword when you specify *long*, *short*, or *unsigned*. On the PC, an *int* without a *long* or *short* type specification, is typically 16 bits, although the increasing popularity of 32-bit compilers is changing that. A *long* integer is usually 32 bits. A *short* integer is usually 16 bits. Quincy uses the 16-bit *short* and *int* and the 32-bit *long*.

Exercise 2.3 illustrates the use of the *int* data type.

EXERCISE 2.3 *The **int** data type.*

```
#include <stdio.h>
main()
{
    int Amount;            /* an int variable */
    Amount = 123;          /* assign a value  */
    printf("%d", Amount);  /* display the int */
}
```

Exercise 2.3 declares an *int* variable named *Amount*. Next, it assigns an integer constant value to the variable. Then it displays the variable on the screen. Exercise 2.3 displays this value on the screen:

123

N O T E

Exercise 2.3 uses the standard library function *printf* to display the integer variable. The *puts* function does not work here, because it displays strings only, and the *Amount* variable is an integer. The *printf* function takes as its first argument a string constant that contains formatting information about the types of the arguments that follow. The string in this exercise specifies that one integer variable follows. The %d token in the string makes this specification. I discuss *printf* in more detail later in this chapter.

When a type has several properties, you can place the type keywords in any sequence. The following declarations are all the same.

```
/* ---- 8 ways to declare an unsigned long integer ---- */
unsigned long Tyler1:
long unsigned Tyler2;
unsigned long int Tyler3;
unsigned int long Tyler4;
long unsigned int Tyler5;
long int unsigned Tyler6;
int unsigned long Tyler7;
int long unsigned Tyler8;
```

Floating Point Numbers

C supports three kinds of floating point numbers, which are distinguished by their precision. Following are declaration examples for all three.

```
float Amount;               /* single precision */
double BigAmount;           /* double precision */
long double ReallyBigAmount;  /* long double precision */
```

Standard C does not specify the range of values that floating point numbers can contain. These ranges depend on the particular implementation of the C language. The standard does define a header file, **float.h**, with global symbols that identify the ranges. Quincy does not implement **float.h** but instead treats all three floating point numbers as the same type with typical double precision. The range is $2.225074 \times 10^{-308}$ to 1.797693×10^{308}.

N O T E

Now that you know about the ranges of floating point numbers, you can forget about them for a while. This book has very little math in it, using only what we need in Chapter 6 to demonstrate some of the standard math functions. If you are mathematically inclined, you already know about precision, mantissas, exponents, scientific notation, and so on. If not, you can write C programs for the rest of your life without having to know any more about math than you do now.

Exercise 2.4 illustrates the declaration and use of the *float* data type.

EXERCISE 2.4 *The **float** data type.*

```
#include <stdio.h>
main()
{
    float realValue;            /* a float variable  */
    realValue = 1.23;           /* assign a value    */
    printf("%f", realValue);    /* display the float */
}
```

Exercise 2.4 declares a *float* variable named *realValue*. Next, it assigns a constant value to the variable. Then it displays the value. The "%f" formatting string tells *printf* to display a float.

Constants

The section after this one explains C expressions, which consist of variables, operators, and constants. You have already learned about variables, and you have used some constants in the exercises. Now let's discuss constants in a C program.

    Constants, in this context, are what some languages call *literals* and others call *immediate* values. They are constant values that you use explicitly in expressions. A constant is distinguished from a variable in two ways. First, it has no apparent compiled place in memory other than inside the statement in which it appears. Second, you cannot address the constant or change its value. Be aware that these constants are not the same as the *const* variable type qualifier that Chapter 5 talks about.

Character Constants

Character constants specify values that a *char* variable can contain. Exercise 2.2 assigned character constants to a *char* variable. You can code a character constant with an ASCII expression—as shown earlier in Exercise 2.2—or as an escape sequence surrounded by single quote characters (apostrophes). The following statements are assignments of character constants to *char* variables.

```
ch1 = 'A';    /* ASCII character constant */
ch3 = '\x2f'; /* character constant expressed as a hex value */
ch3 = '\013'; /* character constant expressed as an octal value */
```

Escape Sequences

The backslash in the second and third examples just shown is an *escape sequence*. It tells the compiler that something special is coming. In this case, \x means that the characters that follow are a hexadecimal number, and \0 means that the characters that follow are an octal number. Other escape sequences—consisting of a backslash and other characters that represent ASCII values—do not have a displayable character (one that you can type and print) in the character set. These escape sequences apply to character constants and string constants, described later. Table 2.2 shows all the escape sequences.

TABLE 2.2 *Constant escape sequences.*

ESCAPE SEQUENCE	MEANING
\a	audible bell character
\b	backspace
\f	formfeed
\n	newline
\r	carriage return
\t	horizontal tab
\v	vertical tab
\\	backslash
\'	quote
\0	null (zero) character
\"	double quote
\0nnn	octal number (nnn) follows
\xhh	hexadecimal number (hh) follows

The backslash-backslash (\\) escape sequence allows you to code the backslash character itself into the constant so that the compiler does not translate it as an escape sequence. The quote (\') and double quote (\") escape sequences allow you to include those characters in character and string constants so that the compiler does not interpret them as the terminating character of the constant itself.

The *newline* (\n) escape sequence is probably the one you will use the most. When a screen output function finds a newline character in the output data, it resets the cursor to the leftmost column on the screen and moves the cursor down one line. It acts like a carriage return on a typewriter.

Integer Constants

An *integer constant* specifies a *long* or *short, signed* or *unsigned* integer value. The value is short by default unless it is outside the allowable range for short integers. Quincy allows signed short integer values of −32767 to +32768, and unsigned short integer values of –65535 to +65536. These are the ranges that you can represent in a 16-bit word.

You can specify an integer constant as a decimal, hexadecimal, or octal value as shown in these statements:

```
Amount = -129;       /* decimal integer constant     */
HexAmt = 0x12fe;     /* hexadecimal integer constant */
OctalAmt = 0177;     /* octal integer constant       */
```

The leading 0x specifies that the constant is a hexadecimal expression. It can contain the digits 0–9 and the letters A–F in mixed upper- or lowercase. A leading zero alone specifies that the constant is octal and may contain the digits 0–7.

You can specify that a constant is *long* or *unsigned* by adding the *L* or *U* suffix to the constant as shown here:

```
LongAmount = 52388L;     /* long integer constant      */
LongHexAmt = 0x4fea2L;   /* long hex constant          */
UnsignedAmt = 40000U;    /* unsigned integer constant  */
```

The suffixes can be upper- or lowercase.

Floating Constants

A *floating constant* consists of integer and fractional parts separated by a decimal point. Some floating constants use *scientific* or *exponential* notation to represent numbers too big or too small to express with normal notation. Here are some examples:

```
Pi = 3.142857142857;     /* regular decimal notation       */
SmallNumber = 1.234E-40; /* 1.234 x 10 to the -40th power  */
BigNumber = 2.47E201     /* 2.47 x 10 to the 201st power   */
```

Floating constants default to the *double* type unless you provide a suffix on the constant like this:

```
FloatNumber = 1.23E10F   /* float constant        */
LongDoubleNumber = 3.45L /* long double constant  */
```

The suffixes can be upper- or lowercase.

Address Constants

When you begin to use pointers in C programs, a subject that Chapter 5 covers, you will use *address constants*. Variables and functions have memory addresses, and C allows you to reference their addresses with address constants as shown here:

```
CounterPtr = &Counter;    /* address of a variable */
FunctPtr = &DoFunction;   /* address of a function */
```

Address expressions of array elements can be non-constant expressions, too, and Chapter 5 discusses them.

String Constants

Exercise 2.1 passed "My first C program," a string constant (also called a *string literal*) to the *puts* function. You code a string constant as a sequence of ASCII characters surrounded by double quote characters. Escape sequences inside the string constant work the same as they do in character constants. Here are some examples of string constants.

```
cp = "hello, dolly";
puts("\nEnter selection: ");
puts("\aError!");
```

The first statement in the example apparently assigns a string constant to a variable. What it is really doing is assigning the *address* of the string constant to a pointer variable (Chapter 5). The compiler finds a place in memory for the string constant and compiles its address into the statement.

The same thing happens in the second and third statements in the example. The compiler passes the addresses of the string constants to the *puts* function.

The string constants in the second and third statements include escape sequences. The second statement's escape sequence is \n, the *newline* character. The third statement's escape sequence is \a, the audible alarm character. It makes a beeping sound from the computer's speaker.

Adjacent string constants concatenate to form a single string constant. This feature allows you to code long string constants on multiple source code lines as shown in Exercise 2.5.

EXERCISE 2.5 *Concatenated string constants.*

```
#include <stdio.h>
main()
{
    puts("This is the beginning of a very long message that\n"
         "spans several lines of code.\n"
         "This format allows a program to build long string\n"
         "constants without going past the program editor's\n"
         "right margin.");
}
```

Expressions

Statements in a function body consist of individual expressions terminated by the semicolon (;) character. Observe that the call to the *puts* function in Exercise 2.5 is terminated by a semicolon. All statements and declarations in C are terminated that way. The statement is not complete until the semicolon appears.

An expression is a combination of constants, variables, function calls, and operators that, when evaluated, returns a value. Following are some typical C expressions.

```
1+2;
Counter*3;
GrossPay-(FICA+GrossPay*WithHoldingRate);
```

By themselves, these expressions do nothing. They return values, but they have no effect because the program does nothing with the values that the expressions return. Expressions such as these take on meaning on the right side of assignment statements, discussed next, or as arguments in a function call (Chapter 3).

The numerical value that an expression returns has a type. The implicit type of an expression depends on the types of the variables and constants that contribute to the expression. Therefore, an expression might return an integer of any size, an address, or a floating point number of any precision.

Each expression also has a logical property associated with its value. If the expression's value is nonzero, the expression is said to return a *true* value. If the value is zero, the expression returns a *false* value. These logical values can be used as *conditions* in program flow control statements, the subject of Chapter 4.

Assignments

An assignment statement assigns the value returned by an expression to a variable. The variable's contents are the value of the expression after the assignment statement. Here are the expressions shown above used in assignment statements:

```
Amount = 1+2;
Total = Counter*3;
NetPay = GrossPay-(FICA+GrossPay*WithHoldingRate);
```

Now the program does something meaningful with the expressions. Each of the assignment statements assigns an expression's returned value to a named variable. In this example, you may assume that the program declared the variables elsewhere. A variable that receives an assigned value is called an *lvalue* because it is on the left side of the assignment. The expression that provides the assigned value is called an *rvalue* because it is on the right side of the assignment. You will learn that this is an important distinction. Not all expressions can be used as *lvalues*. A constant, for example, is an *rvalue* but cannot be an *lvalue*. A variable can be an *lvalue* if it is not a *const* variable, which is discussed in Chapter 5.

The next exercise illustrates how a program would use assignments such as those just shown. To do that, the program declares variables to receive the values returned by the expressions. Declarations of local variables are made in a statement block at the beginning of the block before any statements. You learn more about local and global variables in Chapter 5. Exercise 2.6 declares three integer variables, assigns to those integers the values returned by the expressions, and displays the new values of the integer variables on the screen.

EXERCISE 2.6 *Assignments and expressions.*

```
#include <stdio.h>
main()
{
    /* --- declare three integers --- */
    int HourlyRate;
    int HoursWorked;
    int GrossPay;
    /* --- assign values to the integers --- */
    HourlyRate = 15;
    HoursWorked = 40;
    GrossPay = HourlyRate * HoursWorked;
    /* --- display the variables on the screen --- */
    printf("%d %d %d", HourlyRate, HoursWorked, GrossPay);
}
```

NOTE

When you use Quincy's tutorial mode to run Exercise 2.6, observe that Quincy opens its Watch Window at the bottom of the screen and displays the values of the three integer variables. As you step through the program, you can watch the values change when the assignment statements execute. Many of the exercises use this automatic variable Watch feature in Quincy to assist you with the lesson.

When you run Exercise 2.6, it displays these three values on the screen:

```
15 40 600
```

The first value in the display, 15, reflects the contents of the *HourlyRate* variable. The second value, 40, is *HoursWorked*. The third, 600, is *GrossPay*. This exercise illustrates how a *printf* formatting string specifies more than one format. The three %d tokens are matched by three integer arguments passed to the function.

If you are a mathematician, assignments might look to you like algebraic equations. In some respects, they are almost the same thing, but at other times they are not. Consider this assignment:

```
AmountDue = Dues + Penalty;
```

Before the assignment statement executes, the two sides can be different, and so the assignment statement is not an equation. After the execution, the two sides are the same, and so the assignment statement appears to be an equation. Now consider this assignment statement:

```
AmountDue = AmountDue + 37.43;
```

This assignment statement is never an equation. The two sides can never be equal at any given time.

Comma-Separated Declarations

C permits you to use a comma-separated list of identifiers to declare multiple variables that have the same type. The three declarations in Exercise 2.5 could have been coded this way:

```
int HourlyRate, HoursWorked, GrossPay;
```

Some programmers use the comma-separated identifier notation but put each identifier on a separate line as shown here:

```
int HourlyRate,     /* hourly rate            */
    HoursWorked,    /* number of hours worked */
    GrossPay;       /* gross weekly pay       */
```

This style provides visual separation of the identifiers and allows you to add comments about each variable. There is another advantage to this style. You can use it to group all related variables together. Later, if the requirements of the program call for you to change the type of a number of related variables, you need only make the change on the first line of code in the declaration. The types of all of the others will then automatically be changed.

Operators in Expressions

An expression consists of function calls, variables, constants, and *operators*. The exercises above used some operators. Now you learn what they mean. Operators can be arithmetic, logical, bitwise logical relational, increment, decrement, or assignment operators. Most operators are *binary*, which means that you code the operator between two expressions. The addition operator is binary. Other operators are *unary*, which means that the operator is associated with one expression only. Unary plus and minus operators are examples.

Arithmetic Operators

The C language has two unary and five binary arithmetic operators as shown in Table 2.3. The multiplication, division, and modulus operators have higher precedence than the binary addition and subtraction operators. The unary plus and minus operators are higher than the others. See "Precedence and Order of Evaluation" later in this chapter.

TABLE 2.3 *Arithmetic operators.*

+	unary plus
–	unary minus
*	multiplication
/	division
%	modulus
+	addition
–	subtraction

Following are examples of assignment statements where the expressions on the right side of the assignments use some of the arithmetic operators from Table 2.3:

```
Celsius = 5 * (Fahrenheit - 32) / 9;
Height = Top - Bottom + 1;
Area = Height * Width;
```

Exercise 2.7 uses the first of those expressions to calculate and display Celsius temperatures from Fahrenheit values that you type in. This exercise is also your first use of the standard *scanf* function, which reads keyboard data into program variables.

EXERCISE 2.7 *Assigning an expression.*

```
#include <stdio.h>
main()
{
    int Celsius, Fahrenheit;
    /* --- read Fahrenheit temperature from keyboard --- */
    printf("\nEnter temperature as degrees Fahrenheit: ");
    scanf("%d", &Fahrenheit);
    /* ---- compute Celsius ---- */
    Celsius = 5 * (Fahrenheit - 32) / 9;
    /* ---- display the result ---- */
    printf("Temperature is %d degrees Celsius", Celsius);
}
```

Exercise 2.7 declares two integer variables and uses *printf* to prompt you to type in the temperature. The *scanf* function uses a formatting string with a %d token that specifies integer intput. The second argument to *scanf* is the address of the *Fahrenheit* variable. The & operator immediately ahead of the variable's identifier specifies that you are passing the address of the variable rather than its value. The *scanf* function needs the variable's address so that the function can copy the input integer into the variable. I will discuss the & *address-of* operator in more detail in Chapter 5 when you learn about pointers and addresses.

Observe the formatting string argument to the *printf* function. The %d token is in the middle of an ASCII message. This formatting string causes the nontoken data to be displayed. Tokens in a formatting string begin with the % character. Anything else is not a token and is displayed. The converted values display in place of the tokens in the string.

When you run the program in Exercise 2.7, it displays these messages. The value 75 in this example is what you type. The value 23 is the computed Celsius temperature. You can use other values to see their effects.

```
Enter temperature as degrees Fahrenheit: 75
Temperature is 23 degrees Celsius
```

The modulus % operator returns the remainder of a division when the first expression is divided by the second, as shown in the next example. The example uses a *BitNumber* variable, which contains a number from 0 to the highest bit in a bit array to compute the *ByteOffset* and *BitOffset* variables.

```
ByteOffset = BitNumber / 8;   /* offset to the byte         */
BitOffset = BitNumber % 8;    /* bit offset within the byte */
```

The unary minus operator returns the negative value of the numeric expression that follows it. If the value was already negative, the operator returns the positive value of the expression.

The unary plus operator is redundant and was added to Standard C for symmetry with unary minus. The unary plus operator doesn't change anything. It doesn't make a negative expression positive, for example.

Logical Operators

Logical operators use the true/false properties of expressions to return a true or false value. In C, the true result of an expression is nonzero. When a nonzero value is subjected to a logical operation, the value is converted to one. False values are always zero. Table 2.4 lists the logical operators.

TABLE 2.4 *Logical operators.*

&&	logical AND
||	logical OR
!	unary NOT

Here are some expressions that use logical operators:

```
tf = flots && jets;  /* 1 if flots and jets are both non-zero */
tf = flots || jets;  /* 1 if either flots or jets is non-zero */
tf = !flots;         /* 1 if flots is zero                     */
```

Do not confuse the && and || operators with their bitwise & and | counterparts discussed in the next section.

The && and || logical operators can have more complex expressions on either side than are shown in these examples. They are most often used to form conditional expressions in the C language's *if*, *for*, and *while* program flow control statements discussed in Chapter 4.

Programs often use the unary NOT logical operator (!) to convert a variable's numeric value to its logical true/false property:

```
tf = !!blob; /* 1 if blob is non-zero; 0 otherwise */
```

The expression uses the unary NOT logical operator twice to compound the negation and return the desired one or zero, true or false value associated with the variable's numeric value.

Chapter 5 has exercises that use logical operators within program control flow statements.

Bitwise Logical Operators

The bitwise logical operators perform bit setting, clearing, inversion, and complement operations on the expressions and return the results. Table 2.5 lists the bitwise logical operators.

TABLE 2.5 *Bitwise logical operators.*

&	bitwise AND
|	bitwise OR
^	bitwise exclusive OR
~	one's complement

All but the last of the operators in Table 2.5 are binary operators. The one's complement operator is a unary operator. You may use these operators with integer expressions only. Bitwise logical operators typically are used to set, clear, invert, and test selected bits in an integer variable. Programmers often use bits as on/off switches in programs. Low-level hardware device driver programs often must manipulate bits in the input/output device registers.

The first three operations in Table 2.5 perform bit mask operations as shown in these examples:

```
result = InputCh & 0x80;  /* clear all but most significant bit */
newval = CtrlCh & ~0x80;  /* clear the most significant bit     */
mask = KeyChar | 0x80;    /* set the most significant bit       */
newch = oldch ^ 1;        /* invert the least significant bit   */
```

The second example above also uses the ~ one's complement operator to convert the 0x80 constant to its one's complement, which is 0x7f. This usage emphasizes the bit that is cleared rather than the bits that are not cleared.

Getting ahead of ourselves and anticipating Chapter 4 somewhat, let's consider the following example, which shows a typical use for the bitwise AND operator—testing the setting of bits in a field:

```
if (Field & BITMASK)
    /* at least one of the bits is set */
```

The *if* statement tests the expression inside the parentheses that follow. If the expression returns a true value, the next statement or statement block executes. Otherwise, it is skipped. That's the part that I'll cover better in Chapter 4. For now the usage demonstrates logical AND in a conditional expression. In this example, the program uses the operator to test whether any of the bits in the *BITMASK* variable match the contents of the *Field* variable.

Bitwise Shift Operators

The bitwise shift operators in Table 2.6 shift integer values right and left a specified number of bits. You may use these operators with integer expressions only.

TABLE 2.6 *Bitwise shift operators.*

<<	left shift
>>	right shift

The shift operators return a value that is equal to the leftmost expression shifted a number of bits equal to the value of the rightmost expression, as shown here:

```
NewFld = OldFld << 3;   /* Shift OldFld 3 bits to the left */
MyData = YourData >> 2; /* Shift YourData 2 bits to the right */
```

In these statements, the field on the left of the assignment receives the shifted value. The variables on the right of the assignment are not themselves shifted. Instead, their values contribute to the expression, which returns a shifted value.

Shifting left inserts zero bits into the low order bits of the result. Shifting right propagates the most significant bit. This behavior preserves the signed property of an integer.

Programmers often use the shift left operator to multiply integers and the shift right operator to divide integers when the multiplier or divisor is known to be a power of two.

Relational Operators

Relational operators compare two expressions and return a true or false value depending on the relative values of the expressions and the operator. Table 2.7 shows the six relational operators.

TABLE 2.7 *Relational operators.*

>	greater than
<	less than
>=	greater than or equal to
<=	less than or equal to
==	equal to
!=	not equal to

Relational operators typically are used in conditional expressions for program control flow statements as shown here:

```
while (Counter > 0)   {   /* test Counter for zero */
    /* ... */
}
```

Why do you suppose that C uses == for equality and = for assignment? Other languages, such as BASIC, use the same = operator for both. The reason is that an assignment statement is an expression that returns a value. The following code is valid:

```
if (Amount = 123)
    /* ... */
```

The code looks like a test for equality between *Amount* and the constant value 123, but it is not because it uses the = assignment operator rather than the ==

equality operator. The assignment (*Amount = 123*) is an expression returning the value 123. The *if* program flow statement tests the true/false condition of the expression. This statement would always return a true value because 123, being nonzero, is always true. If the right side of the expression were a variable, then the true/false result of the test would depend on the value in the variable.

The syntax of the two operators and of conditional expressions invites coding errors. New C programmers often code the = operator when they mean to code the == operator. The statement shown above is a valid statement, but because of the potential for confusion, most compilers issue a warning when they see such a statement. The warning says something like "Possibly incorrect assignment."

To eliminate warnings and to make the code's intentions clear, most programmers who want to test the result of an assignment for a true/false condition use one of two ways. The first is shown here:

```
Amount = NewAmount;
if (Amount != 0)
    /* ... */
```

This combination of statements is similar to the way you would code the assignment and test in programming languages that do not treat assignments as conditional expressions. It is clear and unambiguous. No one misunderstands what the code is doing. Once you are experienced and comfortable with C, however, you might prefer this format:

```
if ((Amount = NewAmount) != 0)
    /* ... */
```

This format is more concise than the first one, and many C programmers prefer it. The parentheses are important, however. As you soon learn, the != operator has higher precedence than the = operator. If you omit the parentheses, *NewAmount != 0* is evaluated before the assignment, and *Amount* is assigned the true/false, one/zero result of that test. Without parentheses, the expression works like this one, which has parentheses added to emphasize the default precedence:

```
if (Amount = (NewAmount != 0))
    /* ... */
```

Chapter 5 has exercises that use relational operators within program control flow statements.

Increment and Decrement Operators

C includes several unique operators. Two of them, the ++ *increment* and --
decrement operators, increment or decrement a variable by the value of one.
Table 2.8 shows these operators.

TABLE 2.8 *Increment and decrement operators.*

The increment and decrement operators can be placed before (prefix) or after
(postfix) the variable that they change, as shown in these examples:

```
--Counter;    /* decrement Counter, prefix notation   */
Quantity--;   /* decrement Quantity, postfix notation */
++Amount;     /* increment Amount, prefix notation    */
Offset++;     /* increment Offset, postfix notation   */
```

As used here, the prefix and postfix forms of the operators have the same effect.
But when they are used as part of a larger expression, the two forms have a different meaning. The prefix operators change the variable before it contributes
to the expression, and the postfix operators change it afterward. Exercise 2.8
demonstrates that behavior.

EXERCISE 2.8 *Increment and decrement operators.*

```
#include <stdio.h>
main()
{
    int Ctr, OldCtr, NewCtr;
    OldCtr = 123;       /* OldCtr is 123                  */
    NewCtr = ++OldCtr; /* NewCtr is 124, OldCtr is 124 */
    Ctr = NewCtr--;     /* Ctr is 124, NewCtr is 123     */
    printf("%d %d %d", OldCtr, NewCtr, Ctr);
}
```

Exercise 2.8 declares three integer variables and assigns a value to one of them.
Then it assigns that variable to one of the others but with a prefix increment

operator. The variable is incremented, and the incremented value is assigned to the receiving variable. The third assignment uses a postfix decrement operator. The variable on the right side is decremented but not until after the assignment. The variable on the left side receives the value before the decrement. You can use Quincy's Watch Window to observe these effects as they happen. Exercise 2.8 displays this value on the screen:

```
124 123 124
```

Assignment Operators

It might not be obvious, but the assignment statements you have been learning about in this chapter are themselves expressions that return values. C has a number of assignment statement formats, all of which are shown in Table 2.9.

TABLE 2.9 *Assignment operators.*

=	assignment
+=	addition assignment
−=	subtraction assignment
*=	multiplication assignment
/=	division assignment
%=	modulus assignment
<<=	shift left assignment
>>=	shift right assignment
&=	bitwise AND assignment
|=	bitwise OR assignment
^=	bitwise exclusive OR assignment

Consider first the garden-variety assignment operator that you have been using until now. Each assignment statement itself returns a value. The value that it returns is the value that is assigned to the variable on the left side of the assignment. That behavior makes possible a widely used C idiom that you do not see in other programming languages. This example shows that idiom:

```
FirstTotal = SecondTotal = 0;
```

The effect of this statement is to assign the value zero to both of the variables. Why is this? First, consider the order in which the assignment statements are evaluated. The assignment operator has *right to left associativity*, which means that the expressions are evaluated starting with the rightmost one. That means that *SecondTotal = 0* is evaluated first. That expression returns the result of the assignment, which is zero in this case. When the leftmost expression is evaluated, the zero return from the rightmost expression is assigned to the leftmost variable. It is as if you coded the expression this way:

```
FirstTotal = (SecondTotal = 0);
```

The parentheses are not needed to force the precedence of the rightmost expression over the leftmost expression, because the associativity of the operator takes care of that. Exercise 2.9 demonstrates this behavior.

EXERCISE 2.9 *Assigning assignments.*

```
#include <stdio.h>
main()
{
    unsigned int This, That, Those;
    /* --- assign the same value to three variables --- */
    This = That = Those = 62440;
    /* --- display three unsigned ints --- */
    printf("%u %u %u", This, That, Those);
}
```

The assignment statement in Exercise 2.9 assigns the same value to all three *unsigned int* variables. Exercise 2.9 displays this value on the screen:

```
62440 62440 62440
```

Observe the formatting string in the *printf* function call in Exercise 2.9. The %u tokens specify that the integers are unsigned. If you use the %d token to specify a signed integer as previous exercises do, *printf* treats the 16-bit variables as signed quantities and would display this on the screen:

```
-3096 -3096 -3096
```

How can 62440 and –3096 be the same value? They are both 16-bit quantities with exactly the same bit configuration, that's how. Their hexadecimal value is 0xf3e8. A signed integer's most significant bit, when set, signifies a negative number. In an unsigned number it simply represents the number 32768. Try changing the expression on the extreme left of the assignment from 62440 to 0xf3e8. The results are the same. Change it to 0x8000, and the program displays 32768.

Can you see why the following multiple assignment expression does not work?

```
(FirstTotal = SecondTotal) = 0;
```

Quincy and most other C compilers report an error if you try to code an expression such as this one. The reason is that the leftmost expression (*FirstTotal = SecondTotal*) is not an *lvalue*. It does not represent a variable that the program can modify. It is, instead, an *rvalue* expression—the value of an assignment—which would be whatever is in *SecondTotal* before the statement executes. You cannot assign a value to such an expression. An assignment expression is an *rvalue* and cannot appear on the left side of another assignment operator.

Compound Assignment Operators

The other assignment operators in Table 2.9 are unique to the C language. Called *compound assignment* operators, they are a form of shorthand that provides a more concise way to modify a variable. Consider this simple assignment statement usage, which is common to most programming languages:

```
Total = Total + 3;
```

This statement assigns a value to a variable where the value is the result of an expression that includes the variable itself. C includes a set of compound assignment operators that do the same thing. The statement can be coded this way as well:

```
Total += 3;
```

Each of the other operand assignment operators in Table 2.9 has a similar effect on the variable but with the effects of the assignment's own operator.

Exercise 2.10 *Compound assignment.*

```
#include <stdio.h>
main()
{
    long Total, SubTotal, Detail;
    /* --- initial values --- */
    Total = 10000;
    SubTotal = 90;
    Detail = 5;
    SubTotal *= Detail;     /* compute SubTotal */
    Total += SubTotal;      /* compute Total    */
    /* ----- display all three ----- */
    printf("%ld %ld %ld", Total, SubTotal, Detail);
}
```

Exercise 2.10 displays this message on the screen:

```
10450 450 5
```

NOTE

There is one significant difference between simple and compound assignment. In a simple assignment, such as *A = A + 1*, the *A* expression is evaluated twice; in a compound assignment, such as *A += 1*, the *A* expression is evaluated once. Usually, this difference has no effect on the operation of the program, but if the expression dereferences an address returned from a function, the function would be called twice. Most C programmers intuitively avoid those kinds of side effects. It might not make sense just yet, but put a bookmark in this place. After you've learned about functions (Chapter 3) and pointers (Chapter 5), you might want to return here and reread this note.

Conditional Operator (?:)

The *conditional operator* tests an expression and returns the result of one of two other expressions depending on the true/false value of the first. The operator takes this form:

```
<expression1> ? <expression2> : <expression3>
```

The evaluation tests the first expression. If that value is true, the resulting value is that of the second expression. Otherwise, the resulting value is that of the third expression. Exercise 2.11 demonstrates the conditional operator with a simple algorithm that computes the penalty for overdue dues at 10%.

EXERCISE 2.11 *The conditional operator.*

```
#include <stdio.h>
main()
{
    float AmountDue;  /* amount to be computed   */
    float Dues;       /* dues amount             */
    int Overdue;      /* 1 if overdue, 0 if on time */

    printf("Enter dues amount: ");
    scanf("%f", &Dues);
    puts("0 = on time");
    puts("1 = overdue");
    printf("Which one? ");
    scanf("%d", &Overdue);

    /* --- use conditional operator to compute --- */
    AmountDue = Overdue ? Dues * 1.10 : Dues;

    printf("Amount due: %f", AmountDue);
}
```

When you run Exercise 2.11 it displays the messages shown below. The **35.50** is the amount you enter as dues. The **1** following the *Which one?* message is the response you type to the question. You can try the program with different dues amounts and different responses to the question. Any nonzero response has the same effect as the **1** response.

```
Enter dues amount: 35.50
0 = on time
1 = overdue
Which one? 1
Amount due: 39.050000
```

NOTE
The formatting string that Exercise 2.11 passes to the *scanf* and *printf* functions is "%f", which tells the functions that the data type to read and display is a *float*. Again, the call to *scanf* passes the address of the argument variable rather than the variable itself.

The conditional operator is a shorthand form of the traditional *if-then-else* program flow control operation. The expression just shown can be performed this way as well:

```
if (OverDue)
    AmountDue = Dues * 1.10;
else
    AmountDue = Dues;
```

It can also be performed this way:

```
AmountDue = Dues;
if (OverDue)
    AmountDue *= 1.10;
```

And this way, too:

```
AmountDue = Dues;
if (OverDue)
    AmountDue += AmountDue * 0.10;
```

And so on. As you can see, C is not only the language of choice but also a language of choices.

Comma Operator

Expressions can be separated by commas. Each comma-separated expression is evaluated, and the value returned from the group is the value of the rightmost expression. Exercise 2.12 is an example of this behavior.

EXERCISE 2.12 *Comma-separated expressions.*

```
#include <stdio.h>
main()
{
    int Val, Amt, Tot, Cnt;
    Amt = 30;
    Tot = 12;
    Cnt = 46;
```

continued

EXERCISE 2.12 *Comma-separated expressions (continued).*

```
    /* --- compute Val = rightmost expression --- */
    Val = (Amt++, --Tot, Cnt+3);

    printf("%d", Val);
}
```

Exercise 2.12 displays the value 49 on the screen, which is the value returned by the comma-separated expression.

NOTE Without the parentheses, *Val* would be assigned the value in *Amt* before the increment. This is because the assignment operator has higher precedence than the comma operator. I'll explain just what that means in the next section.

Precedence and Associativity

Operators have two important properties: their *precedence* and their *associativity* (also called *order of evaluation*). These properties affect the results of an expression that contains more than one operator or that might produce side effects. They determine when and if each inner expression in an outer expression is evaluated.

Table 2.10 shows the precedence and order of evaluation of the operators in the C language.

The + and – operators in the second entry in Table 2.10 are the unary plus and minus operators. The ones in the fourth entry are the binary addition and subtraction operators.

The first two entries list some operators that you haven't learned yet. The first entry includes the parentheses operators for function calls—discussed in Chapter 3 and not to be confused with precedence overriding parentheses—and array subscripts and structure members (Chapter 5). The second entry includes the * pointer operator, the & address-of operator, typecast notation, and the *sizeof* operator, all discussed in Chapter 5.

TABLE 2.10 *Operator precedence and order of evaluation.*

PRECEDENCE	OPERATORS	ASSOCIATIVITY
(Highest)	() [] -> .	left-right
	! ~ ++ -- + - * & (type) sizeof	right-left
	6* / %	left-right
	+ -	left-right
	<< >>	left-right
	< <= > >=	left-right
	== !=	left-right
	&	left-right
	^	left-right
	|	left-right
	&&	left-right
	||	left-right
	?:	right-left
	= += -= *= /= %= &= ^= |= <<= >>=	right-left
(Lowest)	,	left-right

Associativity

Operators at the same level in Table 2.10 have equal precedence. The expressions that the operators affect are evaluated in the order specified in the associativity column of Table 2.10. For example, consider this expression:

```
Total = Price - Discount + SurCharge;
```

The binary minus (–) and plus (+) operators have equal precedence, and they have higher precedence than the assignment (=) operator. Therefore, the order of evaluation proceeds left to right starting with the + and – operators according to their associativity. The evaluation computes the value *Price – Discount*, adds *SurCharge* to that value, and assigns the value to *Total*, which sounds like a reasonable computation.

Suppose, however, that you wanted to subtract the sum of *Discount* and *SurCharge* from *Price*. The calculation just shown would not work because of the associativity of the operators. You would need to override the associativity and force the *Discount + SurCharge* expression to be evaluated first. You do this by putting parentheses around the expression:

```
Total = Price - (Discount + SurCharge);
```

Precedence

Similarly, there are times when the default precedence of operators does not produce the desired result. Consider this expression:

```
Total = Price - Discount * SalesTax;
```

The multiplication operator has higher precedence than the subtraction operator. As a result, the expression evaluates *Discount * SalesTax* first and then evaluates the expression where the result from the multiplication is subtracted from *Price*. This is probably not what you want. You probably want to compute *Price – Discount* first and then multiply that result times the *SalesTax* rate. To do that, you override the expression's default precedence by using parentheses, just as you did to override associativity. Here is the same expression corrected to produce the desired result:

```
Total = (Price - Discount) * Tax;
```

When an Expression Is Not Evaluated

The && and || operators evaluate the expressions starting with the leftmost one. As soon as the truth of the total expression is guaranteed, expression evaluation stops. This means that expressions with side effects might not be evaluated, and the side effects might not be realized. Consider this example:

```
if (MoreData() || MoreTime())
    /* ... */
```

If the *MoreData* function call returns a true value, the full expression is assumed to be true, and it is not necessary to call the *MoreTime* function. If the MoreTime function takes some action that other parts of the program depend on, that action—called a *side effect*—does not get taken. Here's another example:

```
while (--aCounter && --bCounter)
    /* ... */
```

If the decrement of *aCounter* produces a zero result, the full expression is assumed to be false, and the balance of the expression is not evaluated—which means that *bCounter* is not decremented.

The conditional operator (?:) behaves in a similar fashion, as shown in this example:

```
Amount = FirstTime ? InitialAmount++ : RunningAmount++;
```

Only one of the second two expressions is evaluated, depending on the true/false value of the first. This means that when *FirstTime* is true, only *InitialAmount* is incremented, and when *FirstTime* is false, only *RunningAmount* is incremented.

Initializers

Declaration of a variable does not put any data in the variable. The exercises so far have placed assignment statements after the declarations to provide initial data values. You can, however, initialize variables with data by providing an initializer as part of the declaration. Exercise 2.13 demonstrates three different variable initializers.

EXERCISE 2.13 *Initializers.*

```
#include <stdio.h>
main()
{
    int Amount = 3;
    char ch = 'A';
    float Value = 1.23;

    printf("%d %c %f", Amount, ch, Value);
}
```

Usually, a variable is initialized each time the declaration is executed. Exercise 2.13 initializes the three variables immediately after the main function begins execution. Variables that are declared inside other functions and statement blocks are initialized every time the function or statement block begins execution. An exception to this is the static local variable that is initialized the first time it is declared and never again. We'll discuss functions and statement blocks in Chapter 3 and static variables in Chapter 5.

Exercise 2.13 displays this message on the screen:

```
3 A 1.230000
```

An initializer takes the form of an assignment statement with the declaration on the left and an expression on the right. If the variable is global or static, the initializing expression must be a constant value—that is, it may not contain any function calls, references to other variables, or increment and decrement operators. It can contain multiple constants and operators, but that's all. Local variables—the kind you've been using until now—may contain any expression as their intializers.

Type Conversion

The various numeric types—characters, integers, long integers, and floating numbers—have different ranges of values because of their sizes and their signed and unsigned properties. What happens when you use them interchangeably? What happens if you assign a *long int* variable to a *char* variable, for example? Or vice versa?

C applies certain rules of *type conversion* in these cases. Numeric types are interchangeable within certain limits. If you assign a variable of a smaller type to one of a larger type, the value is *promoted* to that larger type, and no information is lost. If you assign a variable of a larger type to one of a smaller type, the value is *demoted*, and if the larger value is greater than the smaller type can contain, the demotion includes truncation of the excess data. Some compilers warn you when this can happen unless you use a typecast (Chapter 5) to tell the compiler that you know about it in advance.

Exercise 2.14 illustrates several type conversions in action.

EXERCISE 2.14 *Type conversions.*

```
#include <stdio.h>
main()
{
    char myChar;
    int myInt;
    long myLong;
    float myFloat = 7e4;
    myChar = myInt = myLong = myFloat;
    printf("\n%c (%02x) %d %ld %e",
        myChar, myChar, myInt, myLong, myFloat);
}
```

Exercise 2.14 displays this message on the screen:

```
p (70) 4464 70000 7.000000e+04
```

The program displays the *myChar* variable twice: once as a character and once to show its hexadecimal value. The *myInt* variable reflects the lost data when a *long int* variable with a value greater than can be held in 16 bits is assigned to an *int* variable. The *long int* variable named *MyLong* loses no data when the *float* variable is assigned to it because a *long* can hold the value represented by 7e4, which is 70000.

Console Input/Output

You have been using *scanf* and *printf* in the exercises in this chapter. They read the keyboard and write to the screen in standard C programs. If you are writing a program that you intend to be portable, you will probably use *printf* and *scanf* extensively, because they are the lowest common denominator for console input/output across all implementations of the C language on all computers.

Most commercial C programs do not use *printf* and *scanf*. They use screen and keyboard function libraries associated with the user interfaces of the system on which the program is to be run. There is a small chance that you will never use them again after finishing this book, although many small utility programs run from the command line and do not use exotic user interfaces.

Whether or not you use the standard functions for console input/output, you will use functions such as *sprintf, fprintf, sscanf,* and *fscanf* to format strings and disk file records. Those functions, discussed in Chapters 6 and 7, use the same formatting conventions as *printf* and *scanf* do.

To use *printf* and *scanf,* you must include the **stdio.h** header file in your program outside any function defined by your program and before the first reference to either of the two functions.

printf

The *printf* function accepts a formatting string and a variable number of arguments. The formatting string is written on the screen after the function replaces certain formatting tokens with the contents of the arguments. The function depends on you to specify formatting tokens that match the types of the arguments exactly. The tokens appear in the string in the order that their corresponding arguments appear in the *printf* call's argument list.

Every *printf* formatting token begins with a percent sign and ends with a character that specifies the type of the argument. Until now, the formatting tokens we've discussed have had just those two elements. There can be other parts, however, that qualify the display of the argument. Here is what can follow the % and precede the type specification character.

First, you can have zero or more of the flags shown in Table 2.11 in any sequence.

TABLE **2.11** *Flags in* **printf** *formatting token.*

Flag	Meaning
–	Left-justify the converted argument
+	Precede signed numeric argument with + or –. (If you omit this flag, – precedes a negative argument, but a positive argument displays unsigned.)
space	Prefix a space to an unsigned numeric argument.
#	Alternate form (see Table 2.12).
0	Display numeric types with leading zeros.

The # alternate form flag in Table 2.11 affects the conversion of the argument depending on its type. Table 2.12 summarizes those effects. The type specifier characters are listed in Table 2.14.

TABLE 2.12 *Alternate forms in **printf** formatting token.*

TYPE SPECIFIER	ALTERNATE FORMS
o	1st digit will be 0
x,X	add 0x or 0X prefix
e,E,f	add decimal point
g,G	add decimal point, do not remove trailing zeros

Following the flags (if there are any) and following the % (if there are no flags) can be a minimum width specifier encoded as a number or as an asterisk (*) flag. If the * flag is in the formatting token, it represents an argument (in the argument list) that is the next argument's minimum width. The target argument displays in at least as many characters, padded by spaces on the left or right, depending on whether the − flag in Table 2.11 has been applied.

Next, you can specify the *precision*, which is a period followed by a number that specifies one of the following:

▼ The minimum number of digits that display for the d, i, o, u, x, and X type specifiers

▼ The number of digits to the right of the decimal point for e, E, and f type specifiers

▼ The maximum number of significant digits for the g and G type specifiers

▼ The maximum number of characters to be displayed from a string.

The precision can also be a period followed by an asterisk (*) flag, which corresponds to an argument in the argument list. Using the asterisk flags for the width and precision allows you to dynamically control the display of numbers by using width and precision variables in the argument list.

Next, you may have one of the characters shown in Table 2.13.

TABLE 2.13 *Format qualifiers.*

FORMAT QUALIFIER	MEANING
h	integer is short
l	integer is long
H	double is long

Finally, in a *printf* format token, you have the type specification character as shown in Table 2.14.

TABLE 2.14 *Type specifier characters.*

TYPE SPECIFIER	MEANING
d,i	Signed *int*
o,u,x,X	*unsigned* octal, decimal, hexadecimal *int*
f	*double* as –ddd.ddd
e,E	*double* as –d.ddde-dd
g,G	*double* as –ddd.ddd with trailing zeros removed
c	*int* is converted to *unsigned char*
s	String
p	Pointer to *void*
n	Pointer to *int* to receive the number of characters written
%	The % is displayed

What you have just learned is a lot to assimilate in one lesson. Don't try to memorize it. Use it as a reference when you want to know how use *printf*, *sprintf*, or *fprintf* to format output. Exercise 2.15 illustrates a *printf* call with several formatting tokens in the string.

EXERCISE **2.15** *printf.*

```
#include <stdio.h>
main()
{
    int cnt = 123;
    long amt = 67300;
    unsigned int qty = 40500;
    float tot = 1.765;

    printf( "\ncnt: %+05d"      /* zero-filled, 5-wide int */
            "\namt: %ld"        /* long int                */
            "\nqty: %5u"        /* 5-wide unsigned int     */
            "\ntot: %.4f",      /* double with 4 decimals  */
            cnt, amt, qty, tot);
}
```

Exercise 2.15 displays these messages on the screen:

```
cnt: +0123
amt: 67300
qty: 40500
tot: 1.7650
```

scanf

The *scanf* function also uses a formatting string. As with *printf*, the string uses formatting tokens to specify the types of the input data values. The matching arguments are addresses of the variables that receive the data.

The % may be followed by a decimal maximum field width. Then there may be h, l, or L, with the same meanings as in Table 2.13. Next comes the type specifier character, which is taken from Table 2.14. You can put as much white space as you want between format tokens.

Exercise 2.16 demonstrates the *scanf* function.

```
#include <stdio.h>
main()
{
    int a;
    char b;
    unsigned c;
    printf("Enter int char unsigned: ");
    scanf("%d %c %u", &a, &b, &c);
    printf("%d %c %u", a, b, c);
}
```

Exercise 2.16 displays the three values that you enter in response to the prompt. Enter the values with spaces between them and with no other punctuation as shown in this example:

```
Enter int char unsigned: 123 X 40000
```

getchar **and** *putchar*

The standard *getchar* and *putchar* functions read and write single characters from and to the standard input and output devices, which are usually the keyboard and the screen. The functions are the foundation of many filter programs that process text data files, because a user can redirect the standard input and output devices to input and output disk files. Chapter 7 discusses input/output redirection. Exercise 2.17 uses *getchar* and *putchar* to copy the input to the output, changing all uppercase characters to lowercase.

```
#include <stdio.h>
#include <ctype.h>

main()
{
    int c;
    while ((c = getchar()) != EOF)
        putchar(tolower(c));
}
```

Exercise 2.17 uses several common C idioms. The *while* statement (Chapter 4) controls loops. The statements in the loop—a single *putchar* function call in this case—execute as long as the expression in the *while* statement is true. The conditional expression assigns the *getchar* return value to the *c* variable. The condition tests the result of that assignment to see if it was the EOF value, an identifier defined in **stdio.h** that represents the end-of-file character.

The standard C function *tolower* returns the lowercase equivalent of the argument character. It is defined in **ctype.h** (Chapter 6). When you run the program, it waits for you to type characters. Even though the program is written to display each character when it is read, the buffered nature of the standard input device causes the program to wait until you press the **Enter** key before the program actually reads any keys. You enter EOF and terminate the program by pressing Ctrl+Z.

The *printf*, *scanf*, *getchar*, and *putchar* functions appear many more times as the chapters proceed.

Summary

In this chapter, you learned that a C program consists of functions and variables and how to write a C program with a *main* function. You learned about including header files and putting comments in your program. You learned the C data types, how to declare variables of those data types, and how to assign values to them. You learned about C constants, expressions, operators, and initializers. Finally, you learned how to display data on the screen by using *putchar* and *printf* and how to read data from the keyboard into memory variables by using *getchar* and *scanf*.

Chapter 3

FUNCTIONS

𝒯his chapter is about C functions, the building blocks of a C program. Functions hold the executable code of a program. The entry and exit points of every C program are in the *main* function. The calls to *puts* and *printf* in Chapter 2 demonstrate the top-down organization of a C program. The *main* function calls other functions, each of which returns to the *main* function. Those other functions might—and probably do—call lower functions. Calling a function executes the function immediately. The calling function suspends operation until the called one returns. Functions can accept arguments, and they can return values.

The programmer learns to think of lower functions that are out of sight as trustworthy black box operations that do their jobs. All the standard library functions are in this category. Programmers also develop and acquire function libraries to serve in this capacity. You seldom see the majority of the source code that contributes to the whole of a particular program.

Read this chapter and use the exercises to learn about these subjects:

▼ Designing functions
▼ Function prototypes

▼ Calling functions
▼ Passing arguments
▼ Returning values

The Function

A function has a *function header* and a *statement body*. The function header has three parts: a return type, a name, and a parameter list. The name is unique within the program. It obeys the rules for identifier naming that you learned in Chapter 2. The return value is a C data type. It is one of the data types from Chapter 2, a pointer to one of the types, a pointer to a structure, or a pointer to an array. (I teach about pointers, structures, and arrays in Chapter 5.) The parameter list consists of zero or more variables into which the caller's arguments are copied. The statement body holds the local variable declarations and executable code for the function.

All the exercises in Chapter 2 had *main* functions, and many of them called other functions from the standard library. None of them declared other functions, which is the subject of this chapter.

Remember the *main*

The *main* function is required in all C programs. The system declares it and your program defines it. The *main* function returns an *int* data type and can accept two arguments. If you do not specify what the function returns, the function's definition defaults to a return of an *int* type. The exercises in Chapter 2 define *main* with the default *int* return, and then they return nothing. You will learn the significance of this apparent anomaly in this chapter.

In addition to its default return type, the *main* function has two default parameters—an *int* and a pointer to an array of *char* pointers—yet the *main* functions in Chapter 2 have empty parameter lists. You will learn about *main*'s default parameters in Chapter 5, but, for now, you should know that *main* can choose not to return what it is defined as returning and can define no parameters when arguments are, in fact, passed to it. Other functions are required to adhere to their declarations, but *main* is exempt.

Your program never calls the *main* function. The system's startup procedure calls it to begin running the program. When *main* returns, the system shutdown procedures take over. You do not have to worry about the startup and shutdown procedures. The compiler provides them when you compile and link the program. However, by convention, when the program terminates successfully, it should return an integer with a zero value. Other values are implementation-dependent, although the value −1 usually represents unsuccessful completion of the program. Operating systems often use shell programs that execute programs from a batch command file and include batch operators to respond to the return values from programs. The MS-DOS command-line processor is one such shell program, and UNIX has several.

To get you into the habit of returning values from *main*, all subsequent exercise programs in this book declare *main* with an *int* return value and return something, usually zero, as shown here:

```
int main()
{
    /* ... */
    return 0;    /* successful completion */
}
```

You will learn other ways to use the *return* statement later in this chapter.

Arguments versus Parameters

The caller of a function passes expressions to the function as arguments. The apparently interchangeable terms *argument* and *parameter* appear frequently in the discussions about the values passed. Here is the difference. A function has parameters, which are the variables into which the values passed are copied before the function begins executing. The function prototype declares the parameter types in its parameter list. The caller of a function passes arguments, which are the values returned from expressions to be copied into the function's parameter variables.

Declaring Functions by Using Prototypes

To call a function, you must declare the function first with respect to its return and parameter types. K&R C did not have that requirement. Functions could be declared implicitly by the first reference to them. They were assumed to expect whatever argument types the function call passed and, unless otherwise declared (see "K&R Function Declarations" below), were expected to return signed integers. Standard C has stronger type checking built into the language definition. Before you can call a function, you must tell the compiler the types of the function's parameters and return value. The declaration of a function is called its prototype. Here are examples of function prototypes:

```
unsigned int BuildRecord(char, int);
void GetRecord(char, int, int);
int isMonday(void);
void DoList(int, ...);
```

Unnamed Parameter Types

Observe that the parameter lists in the prototypes contain type specifications with no identifiers for the parameters. You can put parameter identifiers into prototypes, but the identifiers serve as documentation only. They do not have to correspond to the same identifiers in the function definition's parameter list. Some programmers prefer to omit the identifiers. Others prefer to assign mean-ingful parameter identifiers in the prototype to convey the meanings of the parameters to other programmers who read the prototype.

A Typical Prototype

```
unsigned int BuildRecord(char, int);
```

This first prototype is typical. It declares a function named *BuildRecord* with two parameters in its parameter list: a *char* argument and an *int* argument. The function returns an *unsigned int* value. You can see from this example why some programmers prefer to supply identifiers for prototype parameters. Nothing in the prototype just shown gives a clue as to the purpose for the parameters. A more descriptive (and less terse) prototype of the same function would look like this:

```
unsigned int BuildRecord(char RecordCode, int RecordNumber);
```

Functions Returning *void*

```
void GetRecord(char, int, int);
```

This prototype declares a function named *GetRecord* with three parameters of types *char*, *int*, and *int*. (This one is even more obscure than the previous one. Even if you remember the purposes for the parameters, you might easily forget which *int* comes first.) The *void* return type means that the function returns nothing. A *void* function may not return a value, and you may not call it in the context of an expression where it is expected to return a value. For example, you may not call a *void* function from the right side of an assignment statement or as an argument in a function call.

N O T E

The concept of a *void* function appears to be a contradiction. Traditionally, a function is thought to be something that takes arguments, processes them, and returns a value. K&R C did not have *void* functions. Every function was assumed to return an *int* unless it was declared otherwise, *even when the function itself returned nothing*. That was one of the anomalies in the K&R C definition. Other languages, such as BASIC, Pascal, and PL/1, differentiate between functions—which return values—and *procedures* or *subroutines*, which do not. Standard C preserves the classic C tradition by using the *void* function to define a procedure that returns no value.

Functions with No Parameters

```
int isMonday(void);
```

This prototype defines a function with no parameters. The *void* parameter list identifies it as such. You cannot pass arguments to a function with a void parameter list. Functions that accept no arguments must be assumed to get the data that they work on from external sources instead of from arguments passed by the caller.

Functions with Variable Parameter Lists

```
void DoList(int, ...);
```

This prototype contains one integer parameter type and the *ellipse* (…) token. The ellipse identifies a function that accepts a variable number of arguments with unspecified types. The standard library *printf* and *scanf* functions are defined as accepting a variable number of arguments. That is how they can accept different numbers and types of arguments that match the formatting string. There is a special procedure for writing functions with variable argument lists, and Chapter 6 describes it in the discussion about **stdarg.h**.

Functions Returning Nothing and with No Parameters

```
void DoSomething(void);
```

What could be the purpose of a function that takes no arguments and returns no value? In fact, many functions do just that. They apparently have no input and no output. They perform some task, perhaps using data taken from external sources or maintained internally, and post their results externally. All functions have some effect; otherwise, there would be no reason to call them. The caller might invoke the function and not directly benefit from its execution, except when the caller uses an external data item that the called function modifies. An example is a *Beep( )* function that sounds an audible alarm to alert the user. It needs no parameters and has nothing meaningful to return that a caller could use. Its purpose is singular, and its effect is unaltered by external influences. There are many similar examples.

Standard Library Prototypes

The prototypes for all the standard library functions are in their respective header files. That is why you need to include **stdio.h**, for example, before you can call *puts*, *printf*, *scanf*, or any of the other standard input/output functions.

Functions without Prototypes

You can get away without coding a prototype when the function definition itself appears in the code ahead of any call to it, in which case the function definition serves as its own prototype. To preserve the top-down representation of a program's execution, many programmers do not take advantage of this feature. They put prototypes at the beginning of the program and always make the *main* function the first function defined in the program. The exercises in this book follow that convention.

K&R Function Declarations

K&R C did not have function prototypes, but it did provide for function declarations that specified the return type. If a function's definition was elsewhere lower in the program and a higher function called it, the compiler assumed that the program returned an *int* unless there was a function declaration ahead of the first reference to the function—something like this:

```
long GetAddress();    /* --- K&R function declaration --- */
```

The K&R function declaration says nothing about the function's arguments. A caller may pass anything at all. This was the cause of many bugs in K&R C programs.

Contemporary C compilers accept the K&R convention for implicit declaration of a function, but only when you tell the compiler, by setting a compile option, not to enforce strict compliance with ANSI rules, and only for purposes of tradition. The new compilers must continue to compile old programs.

Defining and Calling Functions

You define a function when you write the code for its function header and statement body. All the exercises so far have defined one function, the *main* function. When a function has a prototype, the function definition must match the prototype exactly with respect to the types of its return value and parameters. Exercise 3.1 defines and calls a function that displays a message on the screen.

EXERCISE 3.1 *Defining a function.*

```
#include <stdio.h>

void ErrorMsg(void);  /* function prototype */

int main()
{
    ErrorMsg();        /* call the function  */
    return 0;
}

/* ----- Display an error message ----- */
void ErrorMsg()
{
    printf("\aError!");
}
```

Exercise 3.1 declares a function named *ErrorMsg* in a function prototype. The *ErrorMsg* function returns nothing and accepts no arguments. The *main* function calls the *ErrorMsg* function. The *ErrorMsg* function calls *printf* to sound the audible alarm and display the message "Error!" on the screen. (The \a escape sequence sounds the alarm.) No doubt *printf* calls functions, too, and those functions call functions—all of which illustrates the top-down, hierarchical organization of functions in a C program.

Observe that *ErrorMsg's* prototype has the word *void* in the parameter list, whereas the actual function definition below has an empty parameter list. You can include the *void* in the definition's parameter list if you want, but many programmers do not like it. Dennis Ritchie, the creator of C, calls *f(void)* an abomination. His opinion should carry weight if only because of who he is. That notwithstanding, you *must* put *void* in the parameter list of prototypes for functions that accept no arguments. The compiler requires it. An empty parameter list tells the compiler that the would-be prototype is an old-style K&R function declaration. You *may* put *void* in the function definition's parameter list, but you don't have to.

Returning from Functions

A function stops executing in one of several ways. One way, to be discussed in Chapter 6, is by calling the standard *exit* function, which terminates both the calling function and the program. A function can terminate by falling through the bottom of its definition the way the *ErrorMsg* function in Exercise 3.1 does. A function that terminates that way must be declared as returning *void* because falling through the bottom returns no value. A function can execute the *return* statement from within its body. The *main* function in Exercise 3.1 executes *return* with a value. A *void*-returning function can use the *return* statement with no value. The *ErrorMsg* function in Exercise 3.1 could have been coded this way:

```
void ErrorMsg()
{
    printf("\aError!");
    return;                  /* return from the function */
}
```

The *return* statement can appear anywhere in the function body, as illustrated by Exercise 3.2.

Exercise 3.2 *Returning with the **return** statement.*

```
#include <stdio.h>
void DecideWhen(void);  /* prototype */

int main()
{
    DecideWhen();
    return 0;
}
/* ----- Decide when to return ----- */
void DecideWhen()
{
    int when;
    printf("When to return (0 = now, 1 = later): ");
    scanf("%d", &when);
    if (when == 0)  {
        printf("Returning now");
        return;     /* return from inside the function  */
    }
    printf("Returning later");
    return;             /* traditional return at the bottom */
}
```

Exercise 3.2 prompts you to enter **0** or **1**. Depending on your entry, the program displays a message and returns. Observe that if you enter values other than 0 and 1, the program's behavior is unpredictable. This is a result of the way *scanf* works. The exercise shows that you can return from anywhere in a function by using the *return* statement. Here are the messages that Exercise 3.2 returns when you enter **0** and then run the program again and enter **1**:

```
When to return (0 = now, 1 = later): 0
Returning now
```

```
When to return (0 = now, 1 = later): 1
Returning later
```

Some programming theorists contend that returning from anywhere except at the end of a function is one of several so-called improper programming practices. C permits the usage, and many programmers, including me, find it useful on occasion. There are, however, good reasons for this deprecation of what is a fairly common programming practice. If you always return from the last statement of a function, then you never need to search a function to see under what circumstances it returns. As with all choices in C, use what works best for you.

Exercise 3.2 introduces a new construct: the nested, brace-enclosed statement block. The *if* statement's condition is followed by a left brace character, which starts a statement block. The matching right brace character three lines later closes the statement block. The block contains the statements that execute if the condition tested by the *if* statement is true. A program can return from inside a nested statement block, as the exercise demonstrates.

Returning Values from Functions

Functions that return values do so in their return statement. Both exercises in this chapter have returned a zero value *int* from their *main* functions. Functions that you define in your programs can return values as well. The prototype declares the return value, as Exercise 3.3 shows.

EXERCISE 3.3 *Returning a value.*

```
#include <stdio.h>
int WidthInInches(void);  /* prototype */

int main()
{
    int wd;

    wd = WidthInInches();   /* call a function that */
                            /* returns a value      */
    printf("Width in inches = %d", wd);
    return 0;
}
/* ----- Compute width in inches ----- */
int WidthInInches()
{
    int feet;
    printf("Enter width in feet: ");
    scanf("%d", &feet);
    return feet * 12;
}
```

Exercise 3.3 displays this prompt and then the following message. The value displayed is the value returned from the *WidthInInches* function.

```
Enter width in feet: 37
Width in inches = 444
```

Ignoring Return Values

What happens when you call a value-returning function in a context where no value is expected—where you do not use the return value, do not assign it to anything, nor use it as an argument to another function? Nothing unusual happens, actually. The function executes, and it dutifully returns its value, but the caller can choose to ignore it. In fact, that has been happening since the first exercise in this book. The standard library functions *printf* and *scanf* both return values. *Printf* returns the number of characters displayed, and *scanf* returns the number of input items assigned. The programs have had no use for those values, so they have ignored them.

Passing and Using Arguments

The *WidthInInches* function in Exercise 3.3 is not functionally strong. It has multiple purposes. Sound program design principles call for the definition of functions, each of which has one specific task. The *WidthInInches* function performs two related but independent tasks. First, it reads the width in feet from the keyboard, and then it uses that value to compute the width in inches. A stronger design would break these tasks into separate functions. Then other parts of the program could independently retrieve widths in feet and compute widths in inches without necessarily doing them both at the same time. Strengthening Exercise 3.3 involves breaking the weak function into two stronger functions. One of the two illustrates how you pass arguments to functions, which is the point of this lesson. Exercise 3.4 is the program from Exercise 3.3, improved and strengthened.

EXERCISE 3.4 *Function arguments.*

```c
#include <stdio.h>
/* --- prototypes --- */
int WidthInFeet(void);
int WidthInInches(int);

int main()
{
    int feet = WidthInFeet();       /* initialize variables */
    int wd = WidthInInches(feet);   /* by calling functions */

    printf("Width in inches = %d", wd);
    return 0;
}
/* ----- Read width in feet ----- */
int WidthInFeet()
{
    int feet;
    printf("Enter width in feet: ");
    scanf("%d", &feet);
    return feet;
}
/* ----- Compute width in inches ----- */
int WidthInInches(int wfeet)
{
    return wfeet * 12;
}
```

Ignore everything else that Exercise 3.4 does for the moment, and observe that it declares the *WidthInInches* function differently than Exercise 3.3 did. The prototype specifies in the parameter list that the function expects an *int* argument. The *main* function calls *WidthInInches* and passes an *int* variable argument named *feet*. The program defines *WidthInInches* to match the prototype with respect to the return type and parameter type, but the parameter list must assign an identifier to the parameter. This parameter, named *wfeet*, is a local variable in the *WidthInInches* function. The function call copies the value of the argument into this variable. The *return* statement uses the *wfeet* variable in an expression to compute the return value. The declaration, call, and definition of functions that have parameters are the main lessons that Exercise 3.4 teaches. The program displays the same messages that Exercise 3.3 displays.

The Scope of Identifiers

Exercise 3.4 teaches other lessons in addition to the passing of arguments. First, observe that both the *main* and the *WidthInFeet* functions have integer variables named *feet*. This is correct, because C supports variables with *local scope*. As long as an identifier is declared inside a statement block, that identifier is visible only to the statements in that and lower blocks. Identical identifiers in other blocks outside the function are distinct from the local one. Identical identifiers in higher blocks in the hierarchy are effectively overridden by the lower declaration until the identifier goes out of scope. You will learn more about the scope of identifiers in Chapter 5. The parameter variables declared in a function header are also local to the function. The *WidthInInches* function could just as well have named its parameter *feet*, too.

Initializing with Function Calls

The declarations of the *feet* and *wd* variables in *main* have initializers obtained from calls to the *WidthInFeet* and *WidthInInches* functions. Heretofore, you have seen initializers that contain constant expressions only. Initializers of *automatic* variables, which these two are, can contain any kind of expression that returns a value, including a call to a function. You will learn about automatic variables in Chapter 5.

The Sequence of Initializer Execution

There is another lesson in Exercise 3.4. The second initializer uses the first initialized variable as an argument to the function that the second initializer calls. This tells us that initializers are executed in the top-down order in which they occur in the program.

Passing Several Arguments

Some functions accept more than one argument. For example, a function to compute the volume of a brick-shaped object would need to know the height, width, and depth of the object. Exercise 3.5 is an example of a function with several parameters.

EXERCISE 3.5 *Functions with multiple parameters.*

```
#include <stdio.h>
/* ---- prototype ---- */
double Volume(double, double, long);

int main()
{
    double ht, wd;
    long int dp;

    /* ---- get the brick's dimensions ---- */
    printf("Enter height (x.xx), width (x.xx), depth (x): ");
    scanf("%f %f %ld", &ht, &wd, &dp);

    /* ---- compute and display the volume ---- */
    printf("Volume = %f", Volume(ht, wd, dp));
    return 0;          /*^^^^^^^ call function with many args */
}
/* ---- compute volume of a brick ---- */
double Volume(double height, double width, long depth)
{
    return height * width * depth;
}
```

Exercise 3.5 displays this message in response to your input:

```
Enter height (x.xx), width (x.xx), depth (x): 1.5 2.2 7
Volume = 23.100000
```

Function Calls as Arguments

As with many exercises, I use Exercise 3.5 to teach another lesson in addition to its principal one. This time, the call to the *Volume* function is coded as an argument to the *printf* function. The *printf* function expects a floating point type argument to be passed, and *Volume* returns a double. Therefore, it is perfectly acceptable to use the function call in the context of an expression that would return what the function returns. A more traditional programming language would require a temporary variable, an assignment, and the temporary variable passed as the argument. You can write C programs using that convention if you want—as shown below—but most programmers prefer the more concise code used in Exercise 3.5.

```
double temp;    /* temporary variable */
/* ... */
temp = Volume(ht, wd, dp);
printf("Volume = %f", temp);
```

K&R Function Definitions

K&R C function definitions used different conventions for specifying the types in the parameter list. The list itself provided the parameter identifiers only and not the types. The *WidthInInches* function in Exercise 3.4 could have been defined this way with K&R notation:

```
WidthInInches(wfeet)
{
    return wfeet * 12;
}
```

With nothing more specific about the return or parameter type, the K&R compiler infers that they are of type *int*. Explicit return type definition uses the same convention that Standard C uses. Explicit parameter type specifications, however, are coded in a list of declarations after the parameter list and before the opening left brace of the function's statement body, as shown here:

```
double Volume(height, width, depth)
double height, width;  /* K&R parameter declarations */
long depth;
{
    return height * width * depth;
}
```

K&R C allows you to mix implicit *int* and explicit parameter declarations in the same function definition, as shown here:

```
long AlleyArea(length, width)
long length;                        /* (width is int implicitly) */
{
    return length * width;
}
```

Standard C compilers support the older notation so that programs written before the standard was defined compile correctly. Few programmers, however, use this obsolete notation when writing new programs. You can try it out if you wish. Quincy, originally a K&R C subset interpreter, works with programs that use the older conventions, but I encourage you to use the newer ones.

Pass by Value

C programs pass their arguments to functions *by value* as opposed to *by reference*. This means that a function gets a copy of the argument in its matching parameter. Sometimes, as in the case of large structures, passing by value is inefficient, and you would rather pass a *reference* to the argument than a copy of it. Other times, the function's purpose is to modify the caller's copy of the argument. In both cases, you can build functions that accept the addresses of arguments instead of the arguments themselves. The function declares the parameter to be a *pointer* to the type of the argument, and the caller passes the address of the argument. You are still passing by value, however, except that now you are passing the value of the address of the argument. You learn about pointers and addresses in Chapter 5.

Type Conversions in Arguments and Return Values

Although the return and parameter types of the prototype and the function definition must match exactly, the caller of the function has a bit of leeway. The rules for type conversion that you learned in Chapter 2 apply to function return values and arguments. The compiler appropriately promotes or demotes numeric values to accommodate the expressions that your program provides just as it does in assignments.

Summary

In this chapter, you learned how to design and call functions. You learned that a function's prototype provides its declaration and that all uses of the function as well as the function definition itself must comply with the specification of the prototype. You learned how to define a function by providing a return type, function name, parameter list, and statement body. You learned some of the contexts in which function calls may be used—by themselves, in initializers of local variables, on the right side of expressions, and as arguments to other functions. You learned that function calls pass their arguments by value.

Chapter 4

PROGRAM FLOW CONTROL

This chapter is about C language statements that control the flow of a program's execution. C supports the sequence, selection, and iteration control structures of structured programming as well as the *goto* operation of unstructured programming. You will learn the following subjects in this chapter:

▼ Statement blocks
▼ Selection: *if...else* and *switch*
▼ Iteration: *while, do...while,* and *for*
▼ Loop Control: *break, continue*
▼ Jumping: *goto*
▼ Recursion

Statement Blocks

Every C function has at least one brace-surrounded statement block: the one at the outer level just under the function header. Exercise 3.2 in Chapter 3 included a function with a statement block nested inside the outer statement block. A C function can have many nested levels of statement blocks. These nested blocks are important to C's ability to define groups of statements that execute under controlled conditions. They are also important to the management of local variable scope (Chapter 5).

Nesting Depth

As you develop your programs, be wary of constructs that have too many nested levels of statement blocks. If you indent your statements properly, your code shifts farther to the right of the page as the nested levels increase. Go too far, and the code becomes difficult to read and understand. It is better to reorganize the function and put the deeper nested blocks into their own functions.

Indenting Styles

There are several styles for indenting C code and for placement of the braces that define statement blocks. C, being a free-form programming language, mandates no particular style for braces, indenting, and white space. The style of the exercises in this book reflects the author's personal preference. It is influenced by the style published in K&R. Here are examples of different styles for writing C code:

```
if (a == b)  {   /* then ... endif */
     /* ... */
}

if (a == b)      /* begin ... end */
{
    /* ... */
}

if (a == b)      /* do ... doend */
    {
    /* ... */
    }
```

The comments in these style examples show how C programmers use brace punctuation to express blocks in ways that other languages use keywords. No one style is right, and no one style is wrong. You should strive for consistency, however. Use the same style throughout a program. Eventually, you will find one that you like. If you are modifying someone else's work, use the style that the program uses even if you don't like it. Consistency in code contributes to more readable and, therefore, more maintainable code.

Selection: Tests

The power of the first digital computer was said to be in its ability to make *decisions*, and all of its descendants inherited that ability. Programmers express decisions as tests of a *condition*, which is the true or false value of an expression. Almost every expression returns a value that can be tested for truth. Exceptions are the *void* function that returns nothing (Chapter 3) and the function that returns a *struct* (Chapter 5), which cannot by itself be tested for truth.

An expression is true if its value is not equal to zero; otherwise, it is false. As you learned in Chapter 2, an expression can consist of other expressions and operators and has a true/false condition based on the result of the evaluation of the full expression, which can include arithmetic, logical, relational, and bitwise operations. Any time an expression is used in a context where the program is testing its true/false value, that use of the expression is said to be a condition.

The *if* Statement

C programs use the *if...else* program flow control statement to test conditions and execute one of two statements or statement blocks depending on the condition. Exercise 4.1 illustrates this usage.

EXERCISE 4.1 *Testing with if for Zero.*

```
#include <stdio.h>
int main()
{
    int selection;
    printf("Enter 0 to compute: ");
    scanf("%d", &selection);

    if (selection == 0)
        printf("You chose to compute");

    return 0;
}
```

The expression tested by an *if* statement is always enclosed in parentheses. It can be a complex expression with function calls, operators, variables, and constants.

N O T E

By now you are accustomed to reading code and running exercises either with Quincy or your own C development system. Until now, this book has told you what to expect on the screen when you run the programs. You have reached the point where, in most cases, you can discern for yourself from the code what the programs will display, and you can certainly see it on the screen when you run them. Unless it is either not obvious or critical to the point being made, the book won't belabor the output any further.

There is an important lesson in Exercise 4.1. The *if* statement tests to see if the *selection* variable is equal to zero. This condition is true only if the variable is equal to zero. This might seem backwards. When the variable's value is zero, the expression is true. The explanation for this seeming anomaly is that the full expression includes a comparison with the constant 0. The condition returned by the expression depends on the value of the variable as compared with the constant 0 by the == equality operator; it does not depend on the value of the variable itself. Exercise 4.2 is the same program except that it tests for anything except zero in the variable.

EXERCISE 4.2 *Testing with* ***if*** *for Nonzero.*

```
#include <stdio.h>
int main()
{
    int selection;
    printf("Enter any number but 0 to compute: ");
    scanf("%d", &selection);

    if (selection)
        printf("You chose to compute");

    return 0;
}
```

The *if* statement in Exercise 4.2 uses the variable name alone in the condition. A nonzero value satisfies the test. Many programmers prefer to code such tests explicitly like this:

```
    if (selection != 0)
```

There is no difference between that usage and the usage in Exercise 4.2.

Exercises 4.1 and 4.2 execute one statement if the condition being tested is true. Exercise 4.3 shows that a test executes the statement block that follows immediately when the condition is true.

EXERCISE 4.3 *Conditionally executing a statement block.*

```
#include <stdio.h>
#include <math.h>
int main()
{
    int selection;
    printf("Enter any number but 0 to compute a cube: ");
    scanf("%d", &selection);

    if (selection)  {
        int dim;
        printf("You chose to compute. Enter a dimension: ");
        scanf("%d", &dim);
        printf("%d cubed = %f", dim, pow(3,dim));
        return 0;
    }
    printf("You chose not to compute.");
    return 0;
}
```

Exercise 4.3 has several new lessons. First, it demonstrates that when the *if* statement finds a true condition—when you enter anything other than zero in response to the prompt—all the statements in the following brace-surrounded statement block execute. The indentation of that code emphasizes that relationship, but it has nothing to do with the effect. White space in a C program is for legibility and aesthetics only.

The second lesson is seen in the declaration of the *dim* variable, which occurs at the beginning of the nested block rather than at the top of the function. Such declarations make the variable available only to the statements in the block in which it is declared and to statements in lower blocks. This is an example of the *scope* of identifiers (Chapter 5).

Also observe that Exercise 4.3 includes the **math.h** header file and uses the standard *pow* function to compute the third power of the *dim* variable. If you look into **math.h**, you can see that the *pow* function expects *double* types for its two parameters: yet Exercise 4.3 passes *int* arguments. This usage demonstrates a point made in Chapter 3 that function arguments are subject to the C language rules of type conversion.

Finally, the program does what you learned in Chapter 3 as improper programming. It returns from a place other than the bottom of the function. This book takes no position about the propriety of such code, but the next lesson, which is really about *else*, shows how to remove the so-called improper code.

The *if...else* Statements

In addition to allowing statements that execute when a condition is true, a test can specify that different statements execute when the condition is false. C uses the *else* statement for that purpose, and Exercise 4.4 modifies Exercise 4.3 to use it.

EXERCISE 4.4 *Using else.*

```
#include <stdio.h>
#include <math.h>
int main()
{
    int selection;
    printf("Enter anything but 0 to compute a cube: ");
    scanf("%d", &selection);
```

continued

EXERCISE 4.4 *Using **else** (continued).*

```
    if (selection)  {
        int dim;
        printf("You chose to compute. Enter a dimension: ");
        scanf("%d", &dim);
        printf("%d cubed = %f", dim, pow(3,dim));
    }
    else
        printf("You chose not to compute.");
    return 0;
}
```

The *else* statement executes the statement or statement block that follows when
the condition tested by the associated *if* statement is false. You can have an *else*
statement only when it follows an *if* statement.

The *else if* Statements

Joining a sequence of *if* and *else* statements produces the equivalent of the
ELSEIF operator of other programming languages. It enables you to make a
series of mutually exclusive tests. Exercise 4.5 demonstrates that usage by
implementing a simple screen menu.

EXERCISE 4.5 *Using **else if** for a Menu.*

```
#include <stdio.h>

/* --- prototypes --- */
void DisplayMenu(void);
int GetSelection(void);

int main()
{
    int selection;
    DisplayMenu();                  /* display the menu   */
    selection = GetSelection(); /* get menu selection */
```

continued

EXERCISE 4.5 *Using **else if** for a Menu (continued).*

```
    /* ---- select matching process ---- */
    if (selection == 1)
        puts("Processing Receivables");
    else if (selection == 2)
        puts("Processing Payables");
    else if (selection == 3)
        puts("Quitting");
    else
        puts("\aInvalid selection");
    return 0;
}
/* --- display a menu --- */
void DisplayMenu()
{
    puts("--- Menu ---");
    puts("1=Receivables");
    puts("2=Payables");
    puts("3=Quit");
}
/* --- read a menu selection from the keyboard --- */
int GetSelection()
{
    int sel;
    printf("Enter Selection");
    scanf("%d", &sel);
    return sel;
}
```

Exercise 4.5 displays a menu on the screen and reads the user's selection from the keyboard. Then the program uses the *else if* idiom to test the value of the selection and run an appropriate process, which in this case is simply a message on the screen to indicate which process the user selected.

The *switch...case* Statements

The *switch...case* statements provide a convenient notation for multiple *else if* tests where you test a single integral variable for multiple values. In Exercise 4.5, all the *if* statements test the value of the integer variable named *selection*. The program could have been written with a *switch*. Exercise 4.6 illustrates how to do that.

Exercise 4.6 *The switch...case statement.*

```c
#include <stdio.h>
/* --- prototypes --- */
void DisplayMenu(void);
int GetSelection(void);

int main()
{
    int selection;
    DisplayMenu();                  /* display the menu   */
    selection = GetSelection(); /* get menu selection */

    /* ---- select matching process ---- */
    switch (selection)  {
        case 1:
            puts("Processing Receivables");
            break;
        case 2:
            puts("Processing Payables");
            break;
        case 3:
            puts("Quitting");
            break;
        default:
            puts("\aInvalid selection");
            break;
    }
    return 0;
}
```

NOTE For brevity, Exercise 4.6 does not repeat the *DisplayMenu* and *GetSelection* functions from Exercise 4.5. They are there nonetheless and are in the program on the Quincy diskette. Subsequent exercises apply the same convention.

The condition tested by the *switch* statement must be an integral expression, which means that it can contain operators and function calls. The values tested by the *case* statements must be constant integral values, which means that they can have constant expressions and operators, but they cannot have variables, function calls, or side effects such as assignments and increment and decrement operators. When your tests use these things or when the series of tests involves different variables, use the *else if* idiom.

No two *case* values may evaluate to the same constant value.

The *default* statement is followed by code that executes if none of the *case* values is equal to the *switch* expression. You may omit the *default* statement, but if you include it, there may be only one in a *switch*.

The list of *cases* (including the *default*) is always enclosed by braces. The expression tested by the *switch* is always enclosed in parentheses.

The code executed for each *case* is followed by a *break* statement. If you omit the *break*, execution falls through to the code for the next case in the list. This is not always an error but often is exactly what you want. It allows you to assign the same statements to the same *case*, as shown here:

```
switch (keystroke)   {
    case 'a':
    case 'b':
    case 'c':
        puts("abc");   /* executed for first three cases */
        break;
    case 'd':
        /* ... */
}
```

Iterations: Looping

In addition to making decisions, a program must be able to iterate—repeat sequences of instructions against successive data values. These iterating processes are called loops, and C has three looping statements: *while*, *do...while*, and *for*.

Most programs loop. They operate on a set of data values from a database, the keyboard, a text file, or any of a number of data sources that contain multiple records of similar data. Loop iterations proceed from the first of these records through subsequent ones until there are no more records to process.

Other loops occur within a program's main loop. The program might iterate through arrays once for each input record. Loops can have inner loops, too, such as when an array has multiple dimensions (Chapter 5).

The *while* Statement

The *while* statement tests a condition and if the condition is true, executes the statement or statement block immediately following. When each iteration of the loop is finished, the program returns to the controlling *while* statement, which repeats its test. If the condition is false the first time, no iteration of the loop executes, and execution proceeds with the statement following the loop statements. If the test is true the first time, then something in the loop must, during the first or a subsequent iteration, cause the condition to become false. Otherwise, the loop would never terminate.

In a typical programming mixed (or possibly, confused) metaphor, a loop that is never terminated is said to be a *dead* loop.

N O T E

The program in Exercise 4.6 does not loop. It gets one menu selection from the user, processes it, and exits. More typically, programs process menu selections until the user chooses to exit. Exercise 4.7 uses the *while* statement to execute the program that way.

EXERCISE 4.7 *Iterating with* **while**.

```
#include <stdio.h>
/* --- prototypes --- */
void DisplayMenu(void);
int GetSelection(void);

int main()
{
    int selection = 0;
    /* --- loop until quitting --- */
    while (selection != 3)  {
        DisplayMenu();                  /* display the menu    */
        selection = GetSelection(); /* get menu selection */
        /* ---- select matching process ---- */
        switch (selection)  {
            case 1:
                puts("Processing Receivables");
                break;
            case 2:
                puts("Processing Payables");
                break;
            case 3:
                puts("Quitting");
                break;
```

continued

EXERCISE 4.7 *Iterating with **while** (continued).*

```
            default:
                puts("\aInvalid selection");
                break;
        }
    }
    return 0;
}
```

With one new line of code, Exercise 4.7 turns the earlier program into one that runs until the user says to stop. Note that because of the way the program is written, the first iteration of the loop always runs. The *selection* variable is initialized to zero, and the *while* statement tests it to be equal to 3. Often, a *while* statement does not execute its loop statements at all because the condition is false the first time it is tested.

N O T E   The *selection* variable's initializer is necessary in Exercise 4.7 because local variables are not guaranteed to be initialized to anything in particular, and the random value that *selection* could have on start-up might just be a 3. In Exercise 4.6, the program reads data into the variable before it tests it.

Can you see the potential in Exercise 4.7 for a so-called dead loop? If the user never enters a 3, the *while* loop goes on forever. This, of course, is not a problem in an interactive situation such as this. The user can be expected to understand from the menu display what is required. Eventually, he or she will enter that 3 to get out of the program and on with other things. Dead loops in a program are usually bugs, often occurring in loops that involve no interaction with the user. Here's a simple one:

```
int x = 0, y = 0;
while (x < 3)
    y++;
```

The loop increments *y*, but the *while* statement tests *x*, which never changes. You'll know when you are in such a dead loop. The computer stops dead in its tracks. If you are running the program in Quincy, you can break out of the loop by pressing **Ctrl+Break**, and the Quincy debugger will show you where the loop is. If you have compiled the program with a commercial compiler and are running it under an operating system such as MS-DOS where preemptive interrupts of programs do not occur, you have to reboot the computer.

The *do...while* Statement

Sometimes a loop iteration must execute at least once, regardless of the condition of the variable being tested. The *do...while* statement allows you to write such a loop. Exercise 4.8 demonstrates this behavior.

EXERCISE 4.8 *Iterating with do...while.*

```
#include <stdio.h>
#include <stdlib.h>

int main()
{
    char ans;
    /* --- loop until user is done --- */
    do  {
        int num;
        int fav = rand() % 32;  /* choose a secret number */
        /* --- loop until user guesses secret number --- */
        do  {
            printf("Guess my secret number (0 - 32) ");
            scanf("%d", &num);
            /* --- report the status of the guess --- */
            puts(num < fav ? "Too low"  :
                 num > fav ? "Too high" :
                             "Right");
        } while (num != fav);
        printf("Go again? (y/n) ");
        scanf("%c", &ans);
    } while (ans == 'y');
    return 0;
}
```

Exercise 4.8 has two *do...while* constructs. Each *do* statement is followed by loop statements, which are followed by the *while* test. Observe that the conditions that follow the *while* keywords are in parentheses and are terminated with semicolons.

The difference between *while* and *do...while* is that the test in a *while* happens before each iteration, and the test in a *do...while* happens after each iteration. This behavior is reflected in the way you code the two loops. You code the *while* statement ahead of the loop statements in a *while* test, and after them for a *do...while* test.

The program in Exercise 4.8 computes a random number by calling the **stdlib.h** standard *rand* function. This function returns a random integer between 0 and 32,768. The program reduces this number to one between 0 and 32 by computing the remainder of dividing the random number by 32. Then it goes into a *do...while* loop, letting you guess the number and telling you whether your guess is too high, too low, or right on. When you guess the number, the loop terminates. An outer *do...while* loop lets you exit or guess at another number.

Observe the argument to the *puts* function call. It uses a compound conditional operator to determine which message to pass. The first condition is *num < fav*. If that expression is true, the conditional operator passes the "Too low" message. If that expression is not true, the rightmost expression—which is evaluated and returned for the first conditional operator, is another conditional expression that tests *num > fav*. If that expression is true, the returned value is the "Too high" message. Otherwise, neither condition is true, which means that *num* is equal to *fav*, and the returned value is the "Right" message. This example demonstrates how you can use a series of conditional operators to make a compound test that evaluates to a single value.

The *for* Statement

The C *for* statement is similar to BASIC's FOR operator in that it can control a loop, modifying an initialized variable in each loop iteration. C's *for* statement is more general than BASIC's, however. It consists of three expressions separated by semicolons. The three expressions are surrounded by parentheses and are followed by the statement or statement block that constitutes the iteration. The first expression is evaluated once when the *for* statement executes. Then the second expression is evaluated. If it is true, the iteration executes, and the third expression is evalutated. The loop continues with another test of the second expression, and so on until the second expression is false. This is the format of the *for* statement:

```
for ( <expr1>; <expr2>; <expr3> )
    <iteration>
```

Although the three expressions can be anything you want, including comma-separated expressions, the *for* statement is a convenient notation for a common programming idiom that you could write by using *while* notation this way:

```
<expr1>;
while ( <expr2> )    {
    <iteration>
    <expr3>;
}
```

Consequently, a typical use of the *for* statement is to assign a value to a variable, test that variable for a maximum value, use the variable in the loop iteration, and increment the variable at the end of the iteration. Exercise 4.9 illustrates that usage.

EXERCISE 4.9 *The* **for** *statement.*

```
#include <stdio.h>
#include <stdlib.h>

int main()
{
    int counter;
    for (counter = 0; counter < 10; counter++)    {
        srand(counter+1);
        printf("\nRandom number %d: %d", counter+1, rand());
    }
    return 0;
}
```

The first expression in the *for* loop in Exercise 4.9 assigns a zero value to the *counter* variable. The second expression is a conditional expression that returns true if the *counter* variable is less than 10. The third expression increments the *counter* variable. That combination of expressions in a *for* statement iterates the loop 10 times as long as nothing in the loop modifies the *counter* variable.

Each iteration uses the new value in the *counter* variable as an argument to the **stdlib.h** function named *srand*. This function *seeds* the standard random number generator. Then the program displays the *counter* variable and the next computed random number.

NOTE

If you do not provide a seed value, the *rand* function always starts with a seed of one, and the random number sequence is predictable. You might have observed that the program in Exercise 4.8 always computed the same progression of secret numbers for you to guess. In Chapter 6 you learn how to use values from the **time.h** functions to seed the random number generator to get less predictable results.

The *for* statement is convenient for iterating through the elements of arrays (Chapter 5). Exercise 4.10 introduces that concept.

EXERCISE 4.10 *Using the **for** statement to iterate through an array.*

```
#include <stdio.h>

int main()
{
    int items[5] = {9, 43, 6, 22, 70};
    int i;
    for (i = 0; i < 5; i++)
        printf("\nItem #%d: %d", i+1, items[i]);
    return 0;
}
```

The *items* declaration is a C array. The value inside the square brackets specifies the dimension—the number of elements—in the array. The *items* variable is an array of *int* objects with five elements.

The *for* statement iterates the *i* integer variable from zero through four. Remember that the loop executes only when the second expression in the *for* statement is true, which in this case is so only for the values zero through four. When the integer is incremented at the end of the loop to the value five, the second expression, *i* < 5, is false, and the loop is not executed again.

Array subscripts are relative to zero. Therefore, the elements of an array that has five elements can be accessed with subscripts zero through four. The last argument in the *printf* call, *items[i]*, references the array element of *items* relative to the value in *i*. The expression *items[0]* returns the first element in the array, *items[1]* returns the second, and so on.

Loop Control

Often, a *while*, *do...while*, or *for* loop needs to break out of the loop abruptly regardless of the value of the conditional expression that keeps it going. Other times you need to terminate the current iteration and return to the top of the loop. C provides the *break* and *continue* loop control statements for these purposes.

break

The *break* statement terminates a loop and jumps out of it to the next statement following the iteration code. Be aware that this *break* statement is not the same one used in the *switch...case* selection statement. Exercise 4.11 illustrates the *break* statement from within a *while* loop.

EXERCISE 4.11 *The **break** statement.*

```
#include <stdio.h>
#include <stdlib.h>

int main()
{
    char sel = '\0';
    while (sel != 'q')  {
        printf("\nS-how number, Q-uit: ");
        sel = getchar();
        fflush(stdin);
        if (sel != 's' && sel != 'q')   {
            putchar('\a');
            break;            /* break out of while */
        }
        if (sel == 's')
            printf("\n%d", rand());
    }
    return 0;
}
```

Exercise 4.11 stays in a loop while the *sel* variable is not equal to the character constant 'q'. The user can type any character. As long as that character is 's', the program displays a new random number. If the user presses 'q', the loop terminates normally as the result of the *while* conditional expression. If the user presses any other key, the program sounds the audible alarm with the *putchar('\a')* statement and *break*s out of the loop.

The *break* statement similarly breaks out of *for* and *do...while* loops.

NOTE

Exercise 4.11 calls *fflush* after the *getchar* call. This action flushes the FILE stream identified by the *stdin* argument, which is the standard input device (Chapter 7). If you do not make this call, the carriage return that the user enters for the previous read is read from the input buffer for the current read. Not all C implementations work this way. The ANSI

Standard says that *fflush* is for devices and files that are being written rather than read. Nonetheless, the compiler system with which Quincy was developed (Borland C++ 4.0) requires the *fflush* call, so Quincy, too, requires it.

continue

Sometimes a program wants to return to the top of the loop iteration rather than breaking out. The program in Exercise 4.11 beeps and quits if the user enters an incorrect command code. A more hospitable program would give the user another chance. Exercise 4.12 uses the *continue* statement in place of the *break*. This action terminates the current iteration and returns to the *while* statement to test for the next iteration.

EXERCISE 4.12 *The continue statement.*

```
#include <stdio.h>
#include <stdlib.h>

int main()
{
    char sel = '\0';
    while (sel != 'q') {
        printf("\nS-how number, Q-uit: ");
        sel = getchar();
        fflush(stdin);
        if (sel != 's' && sel != 'q')    {
            putchar('\a');
            continue;
        }
        if (sel == 's')
            printf("\n%d", rand());
    }
    return 0;
}
```

By using the *continue* statement instead of the *break*, the program continues to display the menu until the user presses 'q'.

The *continue* statement works similarly with *for* and *do...while* loops. In a *for* loop, the *continue* statement jumps to evaluate the third expression in the *for* expression list and then to the evaluation of the second. This strategy continues the loop as you would expect it to be continued. In a *do...while* loop, the *continue* statement jumps to the *while* test at the bottom of the loop.

Jumping: *goto*

Everyone who writes about programming deprecates the *goto* statement and cautions you not to use it. Yet most structured programming languages include it. Pascal, originally designed to be a language for teaching structured programming to university students, supports *goto* and statement labels. Often, even those writers who caution against using *goto* suggest programming idioms where *goto* might result in clearer, more efficient programs.

This book takes no position on the use of *goto*. I have written and published a lot of C and C++ code without using *goto*. It has been conclusively proven that any algorithm can be designed with the three control structures of structured programming and without the *goto* statement. Nonetheless, *goto* is a part of the C language, and you should know how it works and decide for yourself if you want to use it.

The *goto* statement references an identifier that must be declared elsewhere in the same function as a statement label. The label can be positioned ahead of any executable statement and is identified with a colon (:) suffix. You can jump in either direction, and you can jump into and out of loops. If you jump into a statement block past declarations that have initializers, the declared objects are in scope, but the initializations have not been made.

Exercise 4.13 shows how you can use *goto* to jump out of an inner loop in a situation where a simple *break* would not work.

EXERCISE 4.13 *The **goto** statement.*

```
#include <stdio.h>

int main()
{
    int i;
    for (i = 1; i < 21; i++) {
        int j, k;
        printf("\nEnter values #%d (0 to quit) ", i);
        for (j = 1; j < 6; j++) {
            scanf("%d", &k);
```

continued

EXERCISE 4.13 *The **goto** statement (continued).*

```
            if (k == 0)
                goto done;
            printf("Entry %d-%d is %d: ", i, j, k);
        }
    }
done:
    puts("\nAll over");
    return 0;
}
```

Recursion

All C functions are *recursive*, which means that a function can call itself, either directly or indirectly, by a lower function that is executing as the result of a call made by the recursive function.

Functions can be recursive because each execution of a function has private copies of its arguments and local data objects, and those copies are distinct from the copies owned by other executions of the same function.

Recursion is used in sorting and parsing algorithms where a *recursive descent* through the data and logic of the program delivers the desired results.

As a programmer, you could be using recursive descent algorithms every time you compile source code. You didn't write them, of course; the programmer who wrote the compiler did. The algorithms parse the source code for correct syntax and evaluate expressions. Perhaps you have wondered how that works.

Exercise 4.14 is a calculator program that evaluates numeric expressions similar to those that you code with the C language. The small calculator implements only addition, subtraction, multiplication, division, and parentheses in an expression. You type the expression into the program with no white spaces. The program evaluates the expression and displays either the result or an error message if you typed an error.

EXERCISE 4.14 *A recursive descent calculator.*

```c
#include <stdio.h>
#include <ctype.h>
#include <stdlib.h>
/* ---- prototypes ---- */
int addsubt(void);
int multdiv(void);
int number(void);
void error(void);

/* --- global expression buffer --- */
char expr[81];
int pos;

int main()
{
    int ans = -1;
    while (ans != 0)    {
        pos = 0;    /* initialize string subscript */
        /* ---- read an expression ---- */
        puts("\nEnter expression (0 to quit): ");
        gets(expr);
        /* --- evaluate the expression --- */
        ans = addsubt();
        if (expr[pos] != '\0')
            error();
        printf("%d", ans);
    }
    return 0;
}
/* ---- top of recursive descent: add/subtract ---- */
int addsubt()
{
    int rtn = multdiv();
    while (expr[pos] == '+' || expr[pos] == '-')    {
        int op = expr[pos++];
        int opr2 = multdiv();
        if (op == '+')
            rtn += opr2;
        else
            rtn -= opr2;
    }
    return rtn;
}
```

continued

EXERCISE 4.14 *A recursive descent calculator (continued).*

```
/* --- highest precedence: multiply/divide ---- */
int multdiv()
{
    int rtn = number();
    while (expr[pos] == '*' || expr[pos] == '/')     {
        int op = expr[pos++];
        int opr2 = number();
        if (op == '*')
            rtn *= opr2;
        else
            rtn /= opr2;
    }
    return rtn;
}
/* ---- extract a number ---- */
int number()
{
    int rtn;
    if (expr[pos] == '(')    {
        /* --- parenthetical expression --- */
        pos++;
        rtn = addsubt();              /* back to top    */
        if (expr[pos++] != ')')       /* must have ')' */
            error();
        return rtn;
    }
    /* --- extract the number --- */
    if (!isdigit(expr[pos]))
        error();
    rtn = atoi(expr+pos);
    while (isdigit(expr[pos]))
        pos++;
    return rtn;
}
/* ---- syntax error ---- */
void error(void)
{
    putchar('\r');
    while (pos-)        /* position error pointer */
        putchar(' ');
    printf("^ syntax error");
    exit(-1);
}
```

The program in Exercise 4.14 scans the expression by subscripting through an array of characters that it reads with the standard *gets* function. The *gets* function reads a string of characters from the keyboard into a character array.

When you type the expression in, the program sets the *pos* subscript to zero and calls the *addsubt* function. Addition and subtraction have the same precedence and, in this calculator, the lowest precedence. The first thing the *addsubt* function does is call the *multdiv* function. Multiplication and division have the same and highest precedence of the operators.

Before doing anything else, the *multdiv* function calls the *number* function to extract the first operand from the expression. That function checks first for a left parenthesis. If it doesn't find one, a number has to be next. The program uses the standard *atoi* function, which converts a string of ASCII digits into an integer. The *number* function returns that integer to the *multdiv* function.

If the *number* function finds a left parenthesis instead of a number, precedence is being overridden, and the function calls *addsubt* to evaluate the parenthetical expression. This is where recursion comes in. The *number* function is executed indirectly by the *addsubt* function, and yet the *number* function itself calls the *addsubt* function.

The recursive call to *addsubt* can initiate other recursive sequences depending on what is in the expression. Eventually they all return to *number*, which returns the value that *addsubt* returned.

The *multdiv* function stores the result from the *number* function. Then it looks for the multiplication and division operators. As long as it finds one of them, it calls the *number* function to get the second operand and computes its result by multiplying or dividing the two values returned by *number*. When it sees no more multiplication or division operators, the *multdiv* function returns its computed value. The *addsubt* function processes the values returned by *multdiv* in a similar way but with the addition and subtraction operators.

When the first execution of *addsubt* returns to the *main* function, the expression evaluation is complete, and the value that it returns is the result of the evaluation.

The program continues to run, getting new expressions from the user until one of them evaluates to zero, telling the program to terminate.

If the evaluation scan finds an error, it calls the *error* function, which displays an error message and terminates the program. It can't simply return, because the error might have occurred at any depth in the recursive descent. A return would cause the expression evaluation to continue from an illogical data position.

One way to deal with such errors so that the program keeps running and gets another expression is to set a global error flag and have each function simpy return if the flag is set. Eventually, the program would get back to the top of the algorithm. That would work, but there is a better way. You will learn about it in Chapter 6 when you read about the standard *setjmp* and *longjmp* functions.

Observe that the *expr* character array and the *pos* subscript variable are declared outside any function. This positioning makes the variables accessible to all the functions in the program. They are in what is called *file scope*. You will learn about this in Chapter 5.

Summary

In this chapter you learned about C statements that manage program flow control. You learned about statement blocks and how they nest. You learned how to use the *if*, *if...else*, *switch...case*, *while*, *do...while*, and *for* flow control statements. You learned about testing and looping and how to use *break* and *continue* to manage loops. You learned about jumping and the *goto* statement and about recursive functions.

Chapter 5

MORE ABOUT DATA TYPES

*T*his chapter adds considerably to what you have already learned about C's intrinsic data types and introduces user-defined data structures, data types, and pointers. You will learn about the following subjects:

▼ The scope of variables and functions
▼ Storage classes
▼ Type qualifiers
▼ User-defined data types
▼ Arrays
▼ Pointer and addresses
▼ Casts
▼ The *sizeof* operator
▼ Command line arguments

Scope

Every identifier in a C program is in global, local, or *file* scope. An identifier's scope determines what statements in the program may reference it—that is, its visibility to other parts of the program. Scope is usually implied by position in the program. The exception is file scope, which must be declared. Variables in different scopes may have the same identifiers.

Global Scope

Some variables and functions have global scope, which means that they can be referenced from anywhere in the program. When a variable is declared outside any function, it is called an *external* variable, and it has global scope by default. The declaration must occur before any references to the variable from within the same source code file, but all functions past that point may reference it. Exercise 5.1 is an illustration of an external variable with global scope.

EXERCISE 5.1 *Global scope.*

```
#include <stdio.h>

int Counter;    /* --- variable with global scope --- */

void AddCounter(int);

int main()
{
    AddCounter(53);
    /* --- reference a global variable --- */
    printf("Counter = %d", Counter);
    return 0;
}

void AddCounter(int incr)
{
    /* --- reference a global variable --- */
    Counter += incr;
}
```

The *Counter* variable in Exercise 5.1 has global scope because it is declared outside any function and is not *static*. Therefore, both the *main* and the *AddCounter* functions can reference *Counter*. Functions themselves have global scope unless they are declared to be *static*.

A variable or function with global scope can be referenced from independently compiled source code modules as long as each module that references one declares it to be *extern*. The *static* and *extern* storage classes are discussed below.

Local Scope

Most of the variables in the exercises of earlier chapters have local scope. They are declared inside functions and are not accessible to the code in other functions. Function parameter variables also have local scope. They are in the scope of and, therefore, are accessible to all the statement blocks in the function.

Variables declared in a statement block are in the scope of that block as well as all lower blocks in the declaring block. Exercise 5.2 illustrates variables with local scope.

EXERCISE 5.2 *Local scope.*

```
#include <stdio.h>

int main()
{
    int i = 123;            /* i is in scope from here down */
    if (i > 0)  {
        int j = 456;        /* j is in scope from here down */
        if (j > 0)  {
            int k = 789;    /* k is in scope from here down */
            /* --- all 3 are in scope --- */
            printf("%d %d %d", i, j, k);
        }
    }
    return 0;
}
```

Variables in different scopes can have the same identifiers. If a variable in a lower scope in a function uses the same name as a previously declared variable, the new declaration *hides* the earlier one from the program until the newer one goes out of scope. A local variable goes out of scope when the statement block in which it is declared completes executing. Exercise 5.3 demonstrates that behavior.

```
#include <stdio.h>

int var = 1;      /* this var is in global scope */

int main()
{
    printf("%d ", var);
    if (var > 0)    {
        int var = 2;         /* hides global var */
        printf("%d ", var);
        if (var > 1)    {
            int var = 3;     /* hides outer local var */
            printf("%d ", var);
        }
        printf("%d ", var);
    }
    printf("%d ", var);
    return 0;
}
```

Exercise 5.3 has five *printf* statements, each one apparently displaying the value of the same variable. The first one references the global *var* because that is the only one that is in scope. The second *printf* references the local var that is initialized with the value 2 and that hides the global *var.* The third *printf* references the local *var* in an inner scope that is initialized with the value 3 and that hides both *var* objects in outer scopes.

When the innermost statement block completes executing, the next outer *var* comes back into scope. Likewise, when its statement block completes, the global *var* comes back into scope. Exercise 5.3 displays the following message on the screen:

```
1 2 3 2 1
```

File Scope

File scope refers to external identifiers that are available only to functions declared in the same *translation unit*, which is the source code file in which they are defined, including any source code files specified by the *#include* statement. The *static* storage class specifier declares identifiers with file scope. Exercise 5.4 illustrates it.

EXERCISE 5.4 *File scope.*

```
#include <stdio.h>

static int Counter;          /* variable with file scope */
static void AddCounter(int); /* function with file scope */

int main()
{
    AddCounter(1940);
    /* --- reference a global variable --- */
    printf("Counter = %d", Counter);
    return 0;
}
/* ---- function with file scope ---- */
static void AddCounter(int incr)
{
    /* --- reference a global variable --- */
    Counter += incr;
}
```

The *Counter* variable and the *AddCounter* function are declared with the *static* storage class specifier. This gives them file scope, which makes them available only to the functions in the translation unit in which they are defined. Exercise 5.4 consists of only one translation unit.

NOTE Most of the exercises in this book have only one translation unit, because Quincy, being an interpreter, does not involve an object file linker. Larger C language development systems support independent compilation of source files, and the *static* storage class specifier hides the identifiers of functions and variables from other source code files linked into the same program.

Storage Classes

Variables can be declared with *storage class* specifiers that tell the compiler how they are to be treated. The storage classes are *auto*, *static*, *extern*, and *register*. The *typedef* keyword is called a storage class for convenience, but it serves a different purpose and is explained later in this chapter.

The *auto* Storage Class

The *auto* storage class specifier identifies a local variable as automatic, which means that each invocation of the statement block in which the variable is defined gets a fresh copy with its own memory space and with re-initialization each time. Local variables are implicitly declared *auto* unless the program declares them otherwise. Use of the *auto* keyword is optional. If you omit it and don't use any other storage class specifier on a local variable, then that variable is automatically automatic. Exercise 5.5 shows how to use the *auto* storage class specifier.

EXERCISE 5.5 *The auto storage class.*

```
#include <stdio.h>

int main()
{
    /* --- auto storage class specifier --- */
    auto int Amount = 500;
    printf("%d", Amount);
    return 0;
}
```

The program in Exercise 5.5 works exactly the same whether or not you include the *auto* keyword in the declaration of the *Amount* variable.

The *static* Storage Class

You learned the meaning of the *static* storage class when you applied it to function declarations and external variables in Exercise 5.4. The *static* storage class has a different meaning with local variables: It is the opposite of *auto*. Although the scope of a *static* local varible begins inside the statement block where the variable is declared and ends when the block terminates, the variable itself retains its value between executions of the statement block. Initializers are effective only for the first time the statement block is executed. Subsequent executions find that the variable has the value it had when the previous execution ended. Exercise 5.6 shows how *static* local variables work.

EXERCISE 5.6 *The **static** storage class.*

```
#include <stdio.h>

int Gather(void);

int main()
{
    int gwool = 0;
    while (gwool < 60)  {
        gwool = Gather();
        printf("\n%d", gwool);
    }
}

int Gather()
{
    static int wool = 50;    /* static local variable */
    return ++wool;
}
```

The *wool* variable in the *Gather* function is a *static* local variable with an initial value of 50. The function increments the variable and returns the incremented value. When you run the program you can see from the output that the returned value is incremented each time, and the *wool* initializer does not have an effect after the first call of the function. If you were to remove the *static* storage class specifier from the declaration, the program would go into a dead loop, displaying the value 51. This is because the *wool* variable would be *auto* rather than *static*, and its intializer would execute every time the function was called, resetting it to 50. The *while* test in the *main* function would never find a true condition, and the program would stay in the loop until you interrupted it manually.

The *extern* Storage Class

The *extern* storage class declares external variables that haven't yet been defined but that the program needs to reference. Usually an *extern* declaration refers to a variable defined in a different translation unit. With Quincy, there are no external translation units, so you could get by without the *extern* storage class by declaring all global variables ahead of any references to them. When you begin programming with complete C language development environments, however, you will find plenty of uses for *extern*.

Exercise 5.7 demonstrates a program that uses an *extern* variable.

EXERCISE 5.7 *The extern storage class.*

```
#include <stdio.h>

void AccumulateAmount(void);

int main()
{
    extern float Amount; /* extern declaration */
    AccumulateAmount();
    printf("Amount: %f", Amount);
}

float Amount;               /* definition of an extern */

void AccumulateAmount()
{
    Amount = 5.72;
}
```

An *extern* variable declaration may be inside or outside the function that references the variable. Either way, the declaration refers to an external variable. If the variable is outside, then all functions in the translation unit can reference the external variable. If it is inside, only the functions that contain an *extern* declaration of the variable can reference the variable.

A program can have several *extern* declarations of a variable but only one definition—a declaration without the *extern* storage class specifier. The definition must appear outside any functions. The declarations and definition may be scattered among many translation units, or all of them may be in the same one. Only one definition/declaration may have an initializer. The initializer may be in the definition or in any of the *extern* declarations, but it may not be in a declaration that is inside a function. If an *extern* declaration has an initializer, then the variable does not need a definition elsewhere in the program, although it may have one. If there is no initializer, then there must be at least one definition.

NOTE Remember from Chapter 1 that a *declaration* declares the format of a variable but does not reserve memory, and a *definition* defines the instance of a variable and reserves memory for it. Often, a variable's definition and declaration are the same C language statement.

Typically, a program declares all *extern* variables in header files that are included by all the translation units. Then it defines each external variable in the C source code module where the variable logically originates.

The *register* Storage Class

A variable declared with the *register* storage class is the same as an *auto* variable except that the program cannot take the variable's address. You learn about variable addresses later in this chapter. Exercise 5.8 demonstrates a register variable.

EXERCISE 5.8 *The **register** storage class.*

```
#include <stdio.h>

int main()
{
    register unsigned int Counter; /* register declaration */

    for (Counter = 100; Counter < 1000; Counter += 50)
        printf("\nCounter: %u", Counter);
}
```

The *register* storage class is a relic in most C implementations. It remains in the language primarily so that older programs still compile. Its purpose was to allow the programmer to specify conditions where the program's performance would be improved if certain local, automatic variables were maintained in one of the computer's hardware registers. It states the programmer's intention to use the variable excessively in the function, which is translated into a suggestion to the compiler to use a register. The compiler can ignore the suggestion.

You cannot take the address of register variables because hardware registers do not have memory addresses on most computers. The address restriction applies even when the compiler chooses to ignore the suggestion and puts the variable in addressable memory.

Effective application of the *register* storage class requires an assembly language programmer's understanding of the processor architecture with respect to the number and kinds of registers available to be used for variables. That understanding would not necessarily apply to a different computer, and so the *register* storage class does not contribute much to a portable program. In addition, contemporary optimizing compilers usually do a much better job than the programmer of selecting which variables can be maintained in registers, although the *register* storage class could conceivably help an aggressive optimizer do its job.

Initial Default Values

Nonlocal and *static* local variables are guaranteed to be initialized with zeros if the program does not explicitly initialize them. Automatic variables are not guaranteed to have any particular initial value when they come into scope. You should either initialize them or assign an initial value to them before you use them.

Type Qualifiers

C includes two *type qualifiers*—keywords *const* and *volatile*—that further define the nature and behavior of variables.

The *const* Type Qualifier

A *const* variable is one that the program may not modify except through initialization when the variable is declared. Exercise 5.9 uses a *const* variable as the upper limit for a loop.

The *const* variable occupies memory, has an address, and may be used in any context that does not or may not modify the contents of the variable. The C *const* variable is primarily intended to allow programmers to identify data in read-only memory. When a variable is qualified as *const*, the compiler prevents the program from modifying the variable's contents. The discussion on pointers later in this chapter has more details about *const*.

EXERCISE 5.9 *The **const** type qualifier.*

```
#include <stdio.h>

int main()
{
    const int Value = 300; /* const declaration */
    int Counter;

    for (Counter = 100; Counter < Value; Counter += 50)
        printf("\nCounter: %d", Counter);
    return 0;
}
```

The *volatile* Type Qualifier

A *volatile* variable is the opposite of a *const* variable. The *volatile* type qualifier tells the compiler that the program could be changing the variable in unseen ways. Those ways are implementation-dependent. One possibility is by an asynchronous interrupt service routine. The compiler must know about such a variable so that the compiler does not optimize its access in ways that would defeat the external changes. Exercise 5.10 shows how you declare a *volatile* variable.

EXERCISE 5.10 *The **volatile** type qualifier.*

```
#include <stdio.h>

volatile int Value = 300; /* volatile declaration */

int main()
{
    int Counter;
    for (Counter = 100; Counter < Value; Counter += 50)
        printf("\nCounter: %d", Counter);
    return 0;
}
```

Suppose that a program posts the address of a variable in an external pointer and that an interrupt service routine elsewhere in the program or in the system modifies the contents of the variable by dereferencing the pointer. If the compiler has optimized the function by using a register for the variable during the interim period in which code used its address, the effects of the interrupt could be lost.

User-defined Data Types

A C programmer can define collections of variables organized in a structure. A structure encapsulates related data into an aggregate. Programs can manipulate structures in ways similar to intrinsic data types. Another data aggregate, called a union, assigns one memory location to several variables, possibly of different types.

You can initialize unions and structures, assign them to one another, pass them to functions, and return them from functions.

Declaring a *struct*

You declare a structure by using the *struct* keyword, giving the structure a name, and declaring the data types that are in the structure, as shown here:

```
struct Date {     /* a struct named Date           */
    int month;    /* data members of the Date struct */
    int day;
    int year:
};
```

A structure declaration begins with the *struct* keyword followed by the name of the structure. The structure consists of variables called the structure's *members*. Their declarations are surrounded by braces. The structure declaration is terminated with a semicolon.

The *struct* declaration does not reserve memory. It merely defines the format of the structure for later use by the program. The structure members can be any valid C type, including other structures.

Defining a *struct* Variable

You define a variable of the *struct* type by providing the *struct* keyword, the structure's name, and a name for the instance of the structure—the *struct* variable—as shown here:

```
struct Date birthday;   /* a Date structure named birthday */
```

Referencing *struct* Members

You reference the members of a structure by providing the name of the structure variable, the dot (.) operator, and the name of the member, as shown here:

```
birthday.day = 24;    /* assign a value to a structure member */
```

Exercise 5.11 declares and uses a *struct* to show you how it all fits into a program.

EXERCISE 5.11 *The **struct** data type.*

```
#include <stdio.h>

/* ---- declare a struct ---- */
struct Date {
    int month, day, year;
};

int main()
{
    struct Date dt;     /* a Date variable */
    /* --- assign values to the struct members --- */
    dt.month = 6;
    dt.day = 24;
    dt.year = 1940;
    /* --- display the struct --- */
    printf("%d/%d/%d", dt.month, dt.day, dt.year);
    return 0;
}
```

Initializing a Structure

Rather than assigning values to each member of a structure variable as Exercise 5.11 does, the program can initialize the variable when it is defined. Exercise 5.12 shows how to initialize a structure variable.

EXERCISE 5.12 *Initializing a **struct**.*

```
#include <stdio.h>

/* ---- declare a struct ---- */
struct Date {
    int month, day, year;
};
```

continued

EXERCISE 5.12 *Initializing a **struct** (continued).*

```
int main()
{
    /* --- an initialized struct --- */
    struct Date dt = { 11, 17, 1941 };
    /* --- display the struct --- */
    printf("%d/%d/%d", dt.month, dt.day, dt.year);
    return 0;
}
```

Structures within Structures

A structure can have other structures as members. Initialization of inner structures uses inner pairs of braces. References to the members of the inner structure include the names of both structure variables, as shown in Exercise 5.13.

EXERCISE 5.13 *Structures within structures.*

```
#include <stdio.h>

/* ---- Date struct ---- */
struct Date {
    int month, day, year;
};

/* ---- Employee struct ---- */
struct Employee {
    int emplno;
    float salary;
    struct Date datehired;
};

int main()
{
    /* --- an initialized Employee struct --- */
    struct Employee joe = { 123, 35500, {5, 17, 82} };

    /* --- display the Employee --- */
    printf("Empl #: %d\nSalary: %0.2f\nDate hired: %d/%d/%d",
            joe.emplno,
            joe.salary,
            joe.datehired.month,   /* reference inner members */
            joe.datehired.day,
            joe.datehired.year);
    return 0;
}
```

Exercise 5.13 declares two structures. The second one has an instance of the first one as a member. When the program initializes an instance of the outer structure, it includes initializers for the inner structure by enclosing them in their own pair of braces.

Referencing the members of the inner structure involves naming both structure variables, each one followed by the dot (.) operator and the member name as the rightmost identifier in the expression.

Passing and Returning Structures to and from Functions

A function can accept a structure as a parameter, and a function can return a structure. For large structures, programmers usually pass structure pointers and let the calling and called functions share copies of the structures. This practice is more efficient because it reduces the overhead of copying large memory segments. It is also safer. Arguments are passed on the stack, which can become exhausted if a program passes many large objects—particularly to recursive functions.

Nonetheless, sometimes you need to pass a private copy of a structure. Perhaps the called function changes the data and the calling function needs to preserve their original values. Other times a function returns a structure. Perhaps that function creates the structure as an automatic variable. The automatic structure goes out of scope when the function returns, so a returned copy is needed. Exercise 5.14 illustrates functions that pass and return structures.

EXERCISE 5.14 *Passing and returning structures.*

```
#include <stdio.h>

struct Date {
    int month, day, year;
};
struct Date GetToday(void);
void PrintDate(struct Date);

int main()
{
    struct Date dt = GetToday();
    PrintDate(dt);
    return 0;
}
```

continued

EXERCISE 5.14 *Passing and returning structures (continued).*

```
/* ---- function that returns a struct ---- */
struct Date GetToday(void)
{
    struct Date dt;
    printf("Enter date (mm dd yy): ");
    scanf("%d %d %d", &dt.month, &dt.day, &dt.year);
    return dt;
}
/* ---- function that has struct parameter ---- */
void PrintDate(struct Date dt)
{
    printf("%d/%d/%d", dt.month, dt.day, dt.year);
}
```

The *union* Data Type

A union looks just like a structure except that it has the *union* keyword instead of *struct*. The difference between unions and structures is that a structure defines an aggregate of adjacent data members, and a union defines a memory address shared by all of its data members. A union can contain only one value at a time, and that value is of the type of one of its members. All of its members occupy the same memory location. The size of a union is the size of its widest member. Exercise 5.15 illustrates the behavior of a union.

EXERCISE 5.15 *The union data type.*

```
#include <stdio.h>

union Holder {
    char  holdchar;
    int   holdint;
    long  holdlong;
    float holdfloat;
};

void DisplayHolder(union Holder, char*);
```

continued

EXERCISE 5.15 *The **union** data type (continued).*

```
int main()
{
    union Holder hld;
    hld.holdchar = 'X';                 /* assign to first member   */
    DisplayHolder(hld, "char");
    hld.holdint = 12345;                /* assign to second member */
    DisplayHolder(hld, "int");
    hld.holdlong = 7654321;             /* assign to third member   */
    DisplayHolder(hld, "long");
    hld.holdfloat = 1.23;               /* assign to fourth member */
    DisplayHolder(hld, "float");
    return 0;
}

void DisplayHolder(union Holder hld, char *tag)
{
    printf("\n---Initialized %s---", tag);
    printf("\nholdchar  %c",  hld.holdchar);
    printf("\nholdint   %d",  hld.holdint);
    printf("\nholdlong  %ld", hld.holdlong);
    printf("\nholdfloat %f",  hld.holdfloat);
}
```

Running Exercise 5.15 demonstrates that changing one of a union's members changes the other members, too. When you assign a value to a particular member, the values of the other members have only coincidental meaning because you are overlaying them with whatever bit configuration represents the assigned member's assigned value. You can observe this behavior by reading the output from the *DisplayHolder* function after each assignment or by using Quincy's Watch window to watch each of the members.

Initializing a *Union*

You can initialize only the first of a union's variables. The initializer is enclosed by braces, and there is only one data value. Its type must be compatible with the first member in the union, as shown here:

```
union Holder hld = {'X'};   /* initialize a union variable */
```

If the first member of a union is a structure, the initialization may include the several expressions that initialize the structure. Exercise 5.16 demonstrates this usage.

EXERCISE 5.16 *Initializing a **union** that contains a struct.*

```
#include <stdio.h>

struct Date {
    int mo, da, yr;
};

union Holder {
    struct Date hdt;
    int hint;
};

int main()
{
    union Holder hld = { {6, 24, 1940} };
    printf("%d/%d/%d", hld.hdt.mo, hld.hdt.da, hld.hdt.yr);
    return 0;
}
```

The *enum* Constant

You can define an enumerated constant by making an *enum* declaration, which defines an enumerated constant data type. An enumerated constant consists of a group of related identifiers, each with an integer value. For example:

```
enum Colors { Red, Green, Blue };
enum Bool { False, True };
```

In these enumerated constants, the first identifer in the brace-surrounded lists is equated with the value zero, the second with 1, and so on. The names must be distinct, and they must not be keywords or any other identifier in the current scope.

You can specify a value for a particular *enum* identifier within the declaration. Immediately following values are incremented starting from that point. For example:

```
enum WeekDay { Sun = 1, Mon, Tue, Wed, Thu, Fri, Sat };
```

In this example, *Sun* is equated to 1, *Mon* is 2, and so on.

You can declare variables of the enumerated type and use enumerated values wherever you can use integers. In fact, the compiler treats them as integer constants. C compilers do not check assignments to enumerated variables to ensure that the assigned expression is one of the enumerated values associated with the type. You can specify an enumerated type in a function's parameter list, but the compiler tests only to see that you pass a value that is or can be converted to an integer. Enumerated types are, in effect, a convenient notation for assigning identifiers to constant integer values.

Exercise 5.17 illustrates the use of an *enum* in a *switch* statement.

EXERCISE 5.17 *The **enum** data type.*

```
#include <stdio.h>

enum Colors { red = 1, green, blue };

int main()
{
    enum Colors col;
    printf("1=Red, 2=Green, 3=Blue. Select: ");
    scanf("%d", &col);
    switch (col)    {
        case red:
            puts("Red");
            break;
        case green:
            puts("Green");
            break;
        case blue:
            puts("Blue");
            break;
        default:
            puts("??");
            break;
    }
    return 0;
}
```

Arrays

All of C's data types can be represented in arrays of one or more dimensions. The dimensions of an array are specified in its definition. An array consists of adjacent instances of variables of the same data type. The variables in an array are called its *elements*. Accesses to the elements of an array are made by providing integer expression *subscripts*.

Declaring Arrays

You declare an array by adding its dimension or dimensions in bracketed expressions after its name. This lesson about is about arrays having one dimension. Here is an example of an array of integers:

```
int Offsets[10];
```

There are 10 integer elements in the array named *Offsets* in the definition just shown. The integers are adjacent in memory. The size of an array is the size of one of its elements times the number of elements in the array. The dimension expression within the brackets may have operators, but it must evaluate to a constant expression. The dimension is relative to one.

Accessing Arrays with Subscripts

To access an element in an array, the program uses the array's identifier followed by a subscript expression in brackets, like this:

```
Offsets[3] = 123;
```

The subscript expression is any expression that evaluates to an integer value. It does not have to be a constant expression. Subscripts are relative to zero, so the example just shown assigns 123 to the fourth element of the *Offsets* array of integers.

Initializing Arrays

You initialize an array by following its definition with a brace-enclosed initialization list. There may be as many initializers as there are elements in the array, as shown here:

```
int Zones[5] = {43, 77, 22, 35, 89};  /* a 5-element array */
```

If you code more initializers than there are elements in the dimension, a compile error occurs. If you code fewer, the remaining elements are initialized with zero values.

By using an empty dimension expression, you can implicitly specify the array's dimension from the number of initializers, as shown here:

```
int Zones[] = {43, 77, 22, 35, 89};  /* 5 elements by default */
```

Exercise 5.18 illustrates a simple array.

EXERCISE 5.18 *An array of integers.*

```
#include <stdio.h>
int main()
{
    int Values[] = {1,2,3,5,8,13,21};
    int i;
    for (i = 0; i < 7; i++)
        printf("\n%d", Values[i]);
    return 0;
}
```

The program in Exercise 5.18 declares an array of seven integers. Then it accesses the array by using a *for* loop that iterates a subscript integer from 0 through 6. Figure 5.1 shows the *Values* array in memory with a subscripted expression that points to the fifth element.

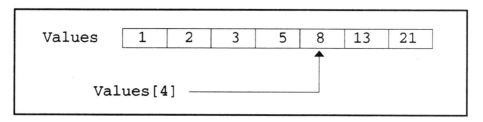

FIGURE 5.1 *An integer array.*

Arrays of Structures

You can build an array of structures and reference the members of each of the array's structure elements by using subscripts. Initialization of the structure uses inner brace-enclosed structure initializers within the brace-enclosed array initializer. Exercise 5.19 demonstrates an array of structures.

EXERCISE 5.19 *Array of structures.*

```
#include <stdio.h>

/* --- Employee record --- */
struct Employee {
    int emplno;
    float wage;
};
/* --- array of Employee records --- */
struct Employee emps[] = {
    { 1, 10.17 },          /* #1 initialized */
    { 2, 15.50 },          /* #2 initialized */
    { 3, 13.00 }           /* #3 initialized */
};

int main()
{
    int i;
    for (i = 0; i < 3; i++)
        printf("\n%d %7.2f", emps[i].emplno, emps[i].wage);
}
```

The *Employee* structure has two members. The *emps* array has three elements. The array initializer contains three inner initializers for the three structure elements in the array. The program iterates through the array with a *for* loop. Finally, the *printf* function call dereferences the structure members with a bracketed subscript expression after the array identifier and before the structure member dot (.) operator.

Multidimensional Arrays

Sometimes an array must have more than one dimension. For example, a grid of numbers reflecting a quarter's monthly revenues by cost center could be implemented as an array with two dimensions. You define a two-dimensional array by adding a second bracketed dimension expression to the definition, as shown here:

```
float Revenues[3][8];   /* 3 months, 8 cost centers */
```

This array is, in effect, three adjacent integer arrays with eight elements each. It is organized in memory that way. The leftmost dimension's elements are adjacent. The first eight elements are followed by the second eight elements, which are followed by the third eight elements.

Exercise 5.20 uses the array just shown to demonstrate how multidimensional arrays work.

EXERCISE 5.20 *Two-dimensional array.*

```
#include <stdio.h>

float Revenues[3][8] = {
    { 45.33, 55.55, 78.00, 37.26, 98.35, 23.55, 45.65, 22.00 },
    { 35.43, 45.45, 79.00, 30.26, 47.55, 34.65, 52.79, 32.50 },
    { 55.37, 75.05, 68.10, 31.27, 62.36, 53.56, 43.68, 24.06 }
};

int main()
{
    int mon, cc;
    for (mon = 0; mon < 3; mon++)    {
        printf("\n%3d ", mon+1);
        for (cc = 0; cc < 8; cc++)
            printf(" %7.2f", Revenues[mon][cc]);
    }
}
```

Figure 5.2 shows how the two-dimensional array is organized in memory and how a subscripted reference accesses one of the array's elements.

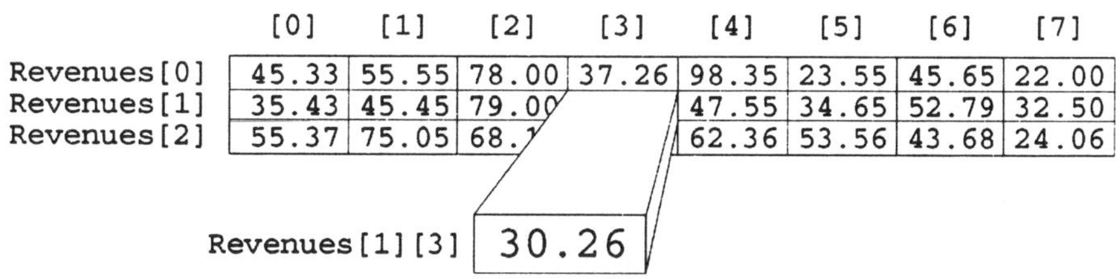

FIGURE 5.2 *Two-dimensional array.*

If any of the inner initializer lists has fewer initializers than there are elements in its corresponding array, the remaining elements are initialized to zero.

You can eliminate all but the outermost pair of braces in an array initialization as long as you provide enough intializers for all of the elements in the inner arrays. The array in Exercise 5.20 could have been initialized like this:

```
float Revenues[3][8] = {
    45.33, 55.55, 78.00, 37.26, 98.35, 23.55, 45.65, 22.00,
    35.43, 45.45, 79.00, 30.26, 47.55, 34.65, 52.79, 32.50,
    55.37, 75.05, 68.10, 31.27, 62.36, 53.56, 43.68, 24.06
};
```

Arrays can have two, three, or more dimensions. Quincy supports up to four dimensions. Standard C imposes no restrictions.

Character Arrays: A Special Case

Character arrays get special treatment with C. The C language has no intrinsic string data type like those of BASIC and other languages. Instead, C supports arrays of *char* variables in special ways. You have seen what appear to be string data types in the string constants that Chapter 2's exercises describe. They are actually null-terminated arrays of characters. Consider the string constant in this example:

```
puts("Hello");
```

The compiler builds an internal character array that, if you could see its declaration, would look like this:

```
char [] = { 'H', 'e', 'l', 'l', 'o', '\0' };
```

The compiler passes the address of the internal array to the *puts* function, which is expecting a pointer to type *char*. Pointers and addresses are discussed in detail in the next section of this chapter. No identifier is assigned to string literals, so the internal representation shown above has none. You cannot declare a *char* array that way yourself—only the compiler can do that. Observe the array's last character constant. It is initialized with the value zero. This is the standard null terminator for a C string constant.

You can initialize a character array with a string constant. Exercise 5.21 shows how that works.

EXERCISE 5.21 *Initializing a char array.*

```
#include <stdio.h>

int main()
{
    char str[] = "Hello, Dolly";
    int i;
    while (str[i] != '\0')
        putchar(str[i++]);
}
```

Pointers and Addresses

Pointers are variables that contain the addresses of other variables and functions. A C program can declare a pointer to any data type, including structures and unions.

A program can use the address of any variable in an expression except for variables with *register* storage class.

A program can assign the address of a variable to a pointer variable. Furthermore, the program can pass the address of a variable as an argument to a function that has a pointer for a parameter.

A program can use the address of a function in an assignment or in an initializer, or as a function argument. A program can call a function through a pointer that has the function's address.

Pointers are an important part of the C language. All arguments are passed to functions by value, which means that a copy of the argument is written into the called function's parameter variable. Programs may not, however, pass arrays by value. Pointers simulate *pass by reference*, in that you can pass the address of an array, structure, or intrinsic data type to be copied into the function's pointer variable parameter. The function's reference to the caller's data is the address of the data in the pointer.

Pointers, addresses, and the notational relationship between pointers and arrays are the source of much of the confusion that new C programmers experience. When I first started programming in C, I made a chart like the code in the following example, hung it on the wall over my desk, and left it there until pointers and addresses were second nature to me.

```
int i, j;  /* int variables                                    */

int *ip;   /* pointer to int variable                          */

ip = &i;   /* assign addr of int variable to pointer to int */

j = *ip;   /* retrieve int that int pointer points to          */

int **ipp; /* pointer to int pointer                           */

ipp = &ip  /* assign address of pointer                        */

j = **ipp; /* retrieve int through pointer to int pointer      */
```

Pointers to Intrinsic Types

You declare a pointer by specifying the type of data that the pointer points to, one or more asterisks, and the name of the pointer itself. The *ip* pointer variable definition in the chart just shown is an example. Remember that pointers are themselves variables. They are usually of uniform size regardless of what they point to, and you can coerce any value into one of them and dereference that value as if it were the address of a variable of the pointer's type. Most compilers, however, warn you if you assign the address of one type to an incompatible pointer type.

NOTE When you are compiling programs for computers such as the PC, that have segmented memory architecture, pointers to functions and pointers to data can have different sizes in programs compiled with different data and code memory models.

Exercise 5.22 demonstrates pointers to C's intrinsic types.

EXERCISE 5.22 *Pointers to intrinsic types.*

```
#include <stdio.h>

int main()
{
    /* --- intrinsic type variables --- */
    char  c = 'A';
    int   i = 123;
    long  l = 54321;
    float f = 3.45;
```

continued

EXERCISE 5.22 *Pointers to intrinsic types (continued).*

```
    /* --- pointers --- */
    char *cp;  /* to char */
    int  *ip;  /* to int  */
    long *lp;  /* to long */
    float *fp; /* to float */
    /* --- assign variable addresses to pointers --- */
    cp = &c;
    ip = &i;
    lp = &l;
    fp = &f;
    /* --- reference the variables through the pointers --- */
    printf("\n%c",  *cp);
    printf("\n%i",  *ip);
    printf("\n%ld", *lp);
    printf("\n%f",  *fp);
}
```

Recall that the *address-of* operator (&) returns the address of the identifier that follows. Assigning the address of a variable to a pointer points that pointer to the variable. Referencing the pointer with the * pointer operator notation dereferences the pointer by returning the value of the variable that the pointer points to.

Pointer Arithmetic

Pointers are integer-like variables. They contain numeric values that happen to be memory addresses. You can add to and subtract integer values from a pointer. The difference between a pointer and a normal integer is that pointer arithmetic adds and subtracts the size of the type that the pointer points to. If you add or subtract 1 to or from a pointer, you really add or subtract the size of what the pointer points to. You can add or subtract integer values to and from pointers returning the new address. You can subtract pointers of the same type from one another. This subtraction returns an integer that represents the number of types between the two addresses. Those are the only arithmetic operations you can perform on pointers. Exercise 5.23 is a small example of pointer arithmetic.

EXERCISE 5.23 *Pointer arithmetic with the increment operator.*

```
#include <stdio.h>

int CountDown[] = { 10,9,8,7,6,5,4,3,2,1,0 };

int main()
{
    int *cdp = &CountDown[0];
    do  {
        printf("\n%d", *cdp);
        cdp++;          /* add 1 to the pointer */
    } while (*cdp);
    printf("\nblast-off");
    return 0;
}
```

The assignment in Exercise 5.23 assigns the address of the first element of the array to the *cdp* pointer. There is a more convenient notation for taking the address of an array, which the next section explains.

The statement that increments *cdp* does not add the integer value 1 to the address in the pointer. Because the pointer is declared with the *int* type, the increment adds the size of *int* variables, which in the Quincy implementation of C is the value 2. You could change the array, the pointer, and the *printf* formatting string all to a different type with a different size—long, for example—and the program would work the same.

You can save some code in Exercise 5.23 by coding the *do* loop this way:

```
do
    printf("\n%d", *cdp++);
while (*cdp);
```

The ++ auto-increment operator has a higher precedence than the * pointer operator, so the expression just shown retrieves what *cdp* points to and then increments *cdp*. To increment the pointer before you retrieve what it points to, you would code the statement this way.

```
printf("\n%d", *++cdp);
```

Sometimes you want to increment what the pointer points to rather than the pointer. For a postfix increment, you would code the expression like this.

```
(*cdp)++
```

The parentheses override the default precedence and apply the increment operator to the variable that the pointer points to. The following notation applies the prefix increment operator to the variable that the pointer points to:

```
++*cdp;
```

Parentheses are not needed in this case because the increment operator applies to the *lvalue* that follows it, which is the variable that the pointer points to.

The above rules apply equally to the auto-decrement operator.

You can use expressions to add and subtract values to and from pointers. Once again, the notation must take into consideration the precedence of the pointer operator and the arithmetic operators. Here are examples using a pointer to type *int*:

```
int ia[] = { 97, 32, 128 };
int i;
int *ip = &ia[0];
i = *ip+1;           /* ip -> 97, returns 98  */
i = *(ip+1);         /* ip -> 97, returns 32  */
```

The first assignment gets the *int* variable that *ip* points to, which is 97, and adds 1 to its value, returning 98.

The second assignment gets the *int* variable one past where the pointer points. The variable in that position has the value 32, which is what the expression returns.

Observe that neither expression changes the values that are stored in the pointer or in the array. They compute values and use those values to form the assignments. The difference between this kind of pointer notation and using auto-increment and decrement operators is that the latter two actually change the value of the pointer or what it points to. Which notation you use depends on what the program is supposed to do. Exercise 5.24 uses a variable to iterate through an array with a pointer.

EXERCISE 5.24 *Pointer arithmetic with expressions.*

```
#include <stdio.h>

float dues[] = {
     30.00,     /* paid quarterly     */
     55.00,     /* paid semiannually  */
    100.00      /* paid annually      */
};

int main()
{
    float *dp = &dues[0];
    int i;
    for (i = 0; i < 3; i++)
        printf("\n%7.2f", *(dp+i));
    return 0;
}
```

Pointers and Arrays

Pointers and arrays have a special and often confusing relationship. The confusion begins when you learn that there are two ways to get the address of an array. The exercises until now used the address-of operator (&) and took the address of the first element in the array. An alternative notation uses just the name of the array. Using the name of an array in an expression is the same as taking the address of the array's first element. The following example compares the notation in Exercise 5.24 with the alternative:

```
float *dp = &dues[0]; /* address of 1st element          */
float *dp1 = dues;     /* address of array (same address) */
```

Carrying that notation further, if you use array address notation with the addition operator and an integer expression, it is the same as taking the address of the array's element subscripted by the expression. For example:

```
float *dp1 = &dues[2]; /* address of 3rd element */
float *dp2 = dues+2;   /*     "      "  "      "   */
```

If the array has multiple dimensions, the same addressing notational conventions apply when you do not include subscripts for all the dimensions. Exercise 5.25 is an example.

EXERCISE 5.25 *Array address notation.*

```
#include <stdio.h>

int calendar[5][7] = {          /* a calendar array            */
     {  1, 2, 3, 4, 5, 6, 7 },
     {  8, 9,10,11,12,13,14 },
     { 15,16,17,18,19,20,21 },
     { 22,23,24,25,26,27,28 },
     { 29,30,31 }
};

int main()
{
    int *cp1 = &calendar[3][2]; /* addr of 4th week, 3rd day */
    int *cp2 = calendar[3]+2;   /*  "    "    "    "    "   "  */
    int *cp3 = calendar[0];     /* addr of array             */
    int *cp4 = calendar[2];     /* addr of 3rd week, 1st day */
    printf("%d %d %d %d", *cp1, *cp2, *cp3, *cp4);
    return 0;
}
```

To add to the confusion, you can dereference what a pointer points to by using array subscript notation. The following usages of a pointer are equivalent:

```
int *ip;       /* a pointer (with address of array assumed)  */
x = *(ip+3);   /* access 4th element of the array            */
x = ip[3];     /* access 4th element with subscript notation */
```

As the example shows, even though *ip* is a pointer, you can use it with array element notation when it points to an array.

If that weren't enough, you can access an element of an array by using pointer notation, as shown here:

```
int ia[10];    /* an array                                   */
x = ia[3];     /* access 4th element of the array            */
x = *(ia+3);   /* access 4th element with pointer notation   */
```

No wonder arrays and pointers confuse new C programmers. You can reduce the level of confusion by sticking with a few basic usage conventions until you are comfortable with the interchangeable nature of pointers and arrays. Exercise 5.26 shows what you can do with pointers and arrays.

EXERCISE 5.26 *Pointers and arrays.*

```
#include <stdio.h>

char msg[] = "\nNow is the time";

int main()
{
    char *cp;    /* a pointer to char    */
    int i;       /* an integer subscript */

    /* --- pointer access, pointer notation --- */
    for (cp = msg; *cp; cp++)
        putchar(*cp);
    /* --- subscript access, subscript notation --- */
    for (i = 0; msg[i]; i++)
        putchar(msg[i]);
    /* --- pointer access, subscript notation --- */
    for (cp = msg; cp[0]; cp++)
        putchar(cp[0]);
    /* --- subscript access, pointer notation --- */
    for (i = 0; *(msg+i); i++)
        putchar(*(msg+i));
    /* --- pointer and subscript access, pointer notation --- */
    for (i = 0, cp = msg; *(cp+i); i++)
        putchar(*(cp+i));
    /* --- pointer and subscript access, subscript notation --- */
    for (i = 0, cp = msg; cp[i]; i++)
        putchar(cp[i]);
    return 0;
}
```

Exercise 5.26 demonstrates six ways that you use combinations of pointers, subscripts, and notation to achieve the same result. All six loops display the same message on the console.

Another variation on this theme occurs when you change the array itself to a pointer to an array. Change the *msg* declaration in Exercise 5.26 to a character pointer like this:

```
 char *msg = "\nNow is the time";
```

The program produces the same results that it did when *msg* was an array. As you can see, the notational conventions for pointers and arrays are virtually interchangeable, which is where more confusion comes in. Until you are used to it, you are never sure what you are looking at when you see an expression that uses pointer and/or subscript notation. It is best at first to use subscript notation with subscripts and pointer notation with pointers. The first two *for* loops in Exercise 5.26 reflect this convention.

The character pointer assignment just shown demonstrates that you can initialize a character pointer with a string constant. As you recall, a string constant is a character array that the compiler builds internally; when you reference it you are referencing its internal address. Therefore, assigning a string constant to a character pointer is really assigning the constant's address to the pointer.

Detractors of the C language consider these pointer/array constructs to be convoluted. Proponents consider them to be among the strengths of C.

Pointers to Structures

Pointers to structures work like other pointers. A structure pointer points to an instance of its structure type. Incrementing and decrementing the pointer changes its address in multiples of the structure's size. You access members in the structure by using the member pointer (->) operator. Exercise 5.27 modifies Exercise 5.19 to use a structure pointer rather than a subscript variable to iterate through the array of structures.

EXERCISE 5.27 *Pointers to structures.*

```
#include <stdio.h>

/* --- Employee record --- */
struct Employee {
    int emplno;
    float wage;
};
/* --- array of Employee records --- */
struct Employee emps[] = {
    {  1, 10.17 },      /* #1 initialized */
    {  2, 15.50 },      /* #2 initialized */
    {  3, 13.00 },      /* #3 initialized */
    { -1, 0      }      /* terminal       */
};
```

continued

EXERCISE 5.27 *Pointers to structures (continued).*

```
int main()
{
    struct Employee *ep = emps;    /* addr of array in ptr */
    while (ep->emplno != -1)    {
        printf("\n%d %7.2f", ep->emplno, ep->wage);
        ep++;
    }
}
```

Observe the two references to the structure members in the *printf* arguments. Instead of the dot (.) structure member operator, they use the member pointer (->) operator. These operators differentiate direct member access to a named structure (.) from indirect member access made through a pointer to a structure (->).

Pointers as Function Arguments

When a function's prototype declares a pointer parameter, callers to the function are expected to pass an argument that is either a pointer or an address. There are two notational conventions for declaring a pointer parameter, as shown here:

```
void ErrorMessage(char *msg);
void ErrorMessage(char msg[]);
```

The two prototypes are the same. Recall that you cannot pass an array as a function argument. The first notation implies that the parameter is a pointer to a character. The second notation implies that the parameter is a pointer to a character array. There is no difference except for the notation. They both work the same way.

If you declare a pointer parameter with array notation and a dimension, the compiler ignores the dimension. The following prototype is the same as the two just shown:

```
void ErrorMessage(char msg[25]);
```

All three prototypes tell the compiler that the parameter is a character pointer. Which form you use is up to you. Many programmers use the first usage because it says exactly what the parameter is, a pointer to a character.

What you pass as an argument can be either a pointer variable or the address of a variable of the pointer's type. Exercise 5.28 demonstrates calls to such functions.

EXERCISE 5.28 *Pointer arguments.*

```
#include <stdio.h>

void ErrorMessage(char *msg);

int main()
{
    char *ep = "Invalid Input";
    char msg[] = "Disk Failure";

    ErrorMessage(ep);          /* pass a pointer variable */
    ErrorMessage(msg);         /* pass an array address    */
    ErrorMessage("Timeout");   /* pass a constant address */
}

void ErrorMessage(char *msg)
{
    puts("\aError!");
    puts(msg);
}
```

Pointer arguments to multiple-dimension arrays must specify the outer dimensions if the function is going to be iterating through the array. The declaration tells the compiler the width of the outer arrays. Exercise 5.29 illustrates this usage.

EXERCISE 5.29 *Pointer arguments to multiple-dimension arrays.*

```
#include <stdio.h>

void DisplayCalendar(int cal[][7]);

int main()
{
    static int calendar[5][7] = {
        {  1, 2, 3, 4, 5, 6, 7 },
        {  8, 9,10,11,12,13,14 },
        { 15,16,17,18,19,20,21 },
        { 22,23,24,25,26,27,28 },
        { 29,30,31 }
    };
```

continued

```
    DisplayCalendar(calendar);
    return 0;
}
/* -- cal argument points to 1st element of
      an array of 7-element arrays -- */
void DisplayCalendar(int cal[][7])
{
    int week, day, date;
    puts("Sun Mon Tue Wed Thu Fri Sat");
    for (week = 0; week < 5; week++)    {
        for (day = 0; day < 7; day++)    {
            date = cal[week][day];
            if (date)
                printf("%2d  ", date);
        }
        putchar('\n');
    }
}
```

Curiously, if you can declare the *DisplayCalendar* function this way, the results
are the same:

```
void DisplayCalendar(int *cal[7]) /* ptr to 7-element array &\*/
```

Returning Addresses from Functions

When a function returns a pointer, it actually returns an address that the calling function can use in an expression where a pointer or address is called for.
Exercise 5.30 is an example of a function that returns an address.

EXERCISE 5.30 *Returning an address.*

```
#include <stdio.h>

int *GetDate(int wk, int dy);

int main()
{
    int wk, dy;
    printf("Enter week (1-5) day (1-7) ");
    scanf("%d %d", &wk, &dy);
```

continued

EXERCISE 5.30 *Returning an address (continued).*

```
    printf("%d", *GetDate(wk, dy));
    return 0;
}

int *GetDate(int wk, int dy)
{
    static int calendar[5][7] = {
        {  1, 2, 3, 4, 5, 6, 7 },
        {  8, 9,10,11,12,13,14 },
        { 15,16,17,18,19,20,21 },
        { 22,23,24,25,26,27,28 },
        { 29,30,31 }
    };
    /* --- return the address of the date --- */
    return &calendar[wk-1][dy-1];
}
```

Observe that the second *printf* call in the *main* function calls *GetDate* with a pointer (*) operator. This notation dereferences the address that the function returns and passes to *printf* the integer that the returned value points to. You can also assign the return value to a pointer variable and then use it to iterate through the array. Exercise 5.31 illustrates that usage.

EXERCISE 5.31 *Iterating with a returned pointer.*

```
#include <stdio.h>

int *GetDate(int wk, int dy);

int main()
{
    int wk, dy;
    int *date;
    printf("Enter week (1-5) day (1-7) ");
    scanf("%d %d", &wk, &dy);
    date = GetDate(wk, dy);
    while (*date != 31)
        printf("%d ", *date++);
    printf("%d ", *date);
    return 0;
}
```

Pointers to Functions

A pointer to a function contains the address of a function, and you can call the function through the pointer. You declare a function pointer using this format:

```
int (*fptr)(void);
```

The pointer's name is *fptr*. This particular pointer points to functions that return *int* and that accept no arguments. The pointer declaration must match those of the functions it points to.

The parentheses around the pointer name and its pointer operator (*) override the default operator precedence. Without them, the pointer definition would look like a prototype of a function that returns a pointer to *int*.

You call a function through its pointer using one of these formats:

```
x = (*fptr)();
x = fptr();
```

The second notation looks just like any other function call. Some programmers prefer to use the first notation because it documents the fact that the function call is through a pointer rather than to a function of that name. Exercise 5.32 demonstrates how a function pointer works.

EXERCISE 5.32 *Function pointers.*

```
#include <stdio.h>

void FileFunc(void), EditFunc(void);

main()
{
    void (*funcp)(void);
```

continued

EXERCISE 5.32 *Function pointers (continued).*

```
    funcp = &FileFunc;
    (*funcp)();
    funcp = &EditFunc;
    (*funcp)();
    return 0;
}

void FileFunc()
{
    puts("File Function");
}
void EditFunc()
{
    puts("Edit Function");
}
```

Exercise 5.32 demonstrates that a function pointer can have different function addresses at different times.

By using arrays of function pointers, you can build *finite state machines* in which the behavior of the program depends on the value of a *state variable* that determines which function executes next. One example of a finite state machine is a table-driven menu manager. Exercise 5.32 shows how such a program might be written.

The four prototyped menu selection functions—which are not shown here (but are in the program on the diskette)—display messages just like the ones in Exercise 5.32. A production program would have custom menu structures and functions to do the work of the menu selections.

EXERCISE 5.33 *A menu manager.*

```
#include <stdio.h>

/* ---- a menu structure ---- */
struct mn {
    char *name;
    void (*fn)(void);
};
/* ---- menu selection functions ---- */
void FileFunc(void);
void EditFunc(void);
void ViewFunc(void);
void ExitFunc(void);
```

continued

EXERCISE 5.33 *A menu manager (continued).*

```
/* ---- the menu ---- */
struct mn menu[] = {
    { "File", FileFunc },
    { "Edit", EditFunc },
    { "View", ViewFunc },
    { "Exit", ExitFunc }
};
main()
{
    /* ---- the menu manager ---- */
    unsigned i, sel = 0;
    while (sel != 4)      {
        for (i = 0; i < 4; i++)
            printf("\n%d: %s", i+1, menu[i].name);
        printf("\nSelect: ");
        scanf("%d", &sel);
        if (sel < 5)
            /* --- call through function pointer --- */
            (*menu[sel-1].fn)();
    }
}
```

Pointers to Pointers

Pointers to pointers can be tricky. You declare them with two asterisks like this:

```
char **cpp;        /* a pointer to a char pointer */
```

It follows that three asterisks declare a pointer to a pointer to a pointer, and four asterisks declare a pointer to a pointer to a pointer to a pointer, and so on. You can deal with that level of complexity after you have familiarized yourself with the simplest case. This book addresses pointers to pointers and goes no deeper than that.

You initialize a pointer to a pointer with the address of a pointer, like this:

```
char c = 'A';        /* a char variable                */
char *cp = &c;       /* a pointer to a char variable */
char **cpp = &cp;    /* a pointer to a pointer        */
```

You can use a pointer to a pointer to access either the pointer that it points to or the data item that the pointed-to pointer points to. Read that last sentence carefully. Here are examples using the pointers just defined:

```
char *cp1 = *cpp; /* retrieve the pointer pointed to        */
char c1 = **cpp;  /* retrieve the char pointed to indirectly */
```

You might well wonder how you would use such constructs. Pointers to pointers can be used to allow a called function to modify a local pointer and to manage arrays of pointers. The latter usage is addressed in the next discussion. Exercise 5.34 demonstrates the former.

EXERCISE 5.34 *Pointers to pointers.*

```
#include <stdio.h>

void FindCredit(float **fpp);

int main()
{
    float vals[] = { 34.23, 67.33, 46.44, -99.22, 85.56, 0 };
    float *fp = vals;
    FindCredit(&fp);
    printf("%f", *fp);
    return 0;
}

void FindCredit(float **fpp)
{
    while (**fpp != 0)
        if (**fpp < 0)
            break;
        else
            (*fpp)++;
}
```

Exercise 5.34 initializes the *fp* pointer with the address of an array and passes the address of the pointer to the *FindCredit* function, which is expecting a pointer to a pointer. *FindCredit* dereferences the array values indirectly with the **fpp* expression. To iterate through the array in search of a negative value, *FindCredit* increments the caller's pointer to the array rather than its own local pointer to the caller's pointer. The *(*fpp)++* statement says to increment what the pointer parameter points to, which in this case is a pointer in the caller's scope. When *FindCredit* returns, the *fp* pointer in *main*—the caller—points to the negative value in the table.

Pointers to Arrays of Pointers

Another use of pointers to pointers is to manage arrays of pointers. Some programmers prefer to use arrays of pointers rather than multiple-dimension arrays. One common use is to point to a table of strings, as shown in Exercise 5.35.

EXERCISE 5.35 *Pointers to arrays of pointers.*

```
#include <stdio.h>

char *Names[] = {  /* array of char pointers */
    "Bill",         /* initialized with names */
    "Sam",
    "Jim",
    "Paul",
    "Charles",
    "Donald",
    NULL            /* NULL (0) pointer        */
};

int main()
{
    char **nm = Names;  /* pointer to pointer      */
    while (*nm != NULL)
        puts(*nm++);    /* point to next pointer */
    return 0;
}
```

Exercise 5.35 initializes the *nm* pointer to the address of the *Names* array, which is an array of character pointers. Each *puts* call passes the character pointer that the *nm* pointer points to and then increments the pointer to the next element (pointer) in the array. Observe that the syntax for doing that is **nm++*, which retrieves what the pointer points to and then increments the pointer itself. Figure 5.3 illustrates the relationship between the pointers in the *Names* array, what they point to, and the *nm* pointer to the array.

Observe the *NULL* identifier assigned to the last element of the array and tested for in the *while* loop. *NULL* is a symbol equated to a zero-value pointer in **stdio.h**. It is frequently used as a terminal symbol in arrays of pointers. By using it this way, you can add elements to and remove elements from the array without having to change the code that searches the array. The code adjusts to the new array because it iterates through the array until it finds the *NULL* value.

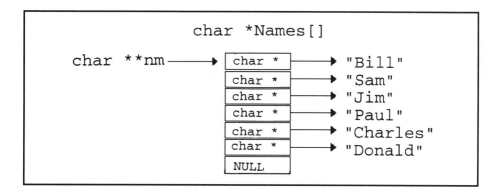

FIGURE 5.3 *Pointer to an array of **char** pointers.*

Pointers to *const* Variables

When you declare a pointer that points to a *const* variable, you are saying that the program cannot modify the variable through the pointer. The declaration looks like this:

```
const char *str;
```

Any reference to the character data that *str* points to must be read-only. There are a number of implications of this usage. First, you may not assign the address of a *const* variable to a pointer unless the pointer is declared as just shown. Furthermore, you may not pass the address of a *const* variable as an argument to a function where the matching parameter is declared to be a pointer to a non-*const* variable. The following code illustrates this usage:

```
const char s1[] = "abcde"; /* const variable, cannot change  */
char *cp1 = s1;            /* error, pointer is not to const */
const char *cp2 = s1;      /* ok, pointer is to const        */
void foo(char *ps);
void bar(const char *ps);
foo(s1);                   /* error, parameter is not const  */
bar(s1);                   /* ok, parameter is const         */
```

A typical use of a pointer to *const* is to qualify a function parameter so that the compiler prevents the function from trying to change the caller's copy of the variable and to allow callers to pass addresses of *const* variables. Exercise 5.36 implements the standard *strcpy* function to demonstrate how this works.

EXERCISE 5.36 *const pointer arguments.*

```
#include <stdio.h>
#include <string.h>

char *strcpy(char *s1, const char *s2)   /* const argument */
{
    char *s = s1;
    while ((*s1++ = *s2++) != '\0')
        ;
    return s;
}

int main()
{
    char rcv[25];
    const char snd[] = "Hello, Dolly";
    strcpy(rcv, snd);
    puts(rcv);
    return 0;
}
```

The call to *strcpy* works because the first parameter is non-*const,* the second parameter is *const,* and the arguments match. The function modifies what the first argument points to by reading the second argument. The function would still work if both arguments were non-*const,* but it is a compile-time error to pass a *const* argument for the first parameter. The non-*const* property of the parameter indicates that the function could modify what the pointer points to, so the compiler does not permit it to point to a *const* variable.

As a rule, declare pointer function parameters as pointing to *const* when the function needs read-only access to the argument. This permits you to call the function passing the address of *const* variables.

N O T E

Exercise 5.36 defines the Standard C *strcpy* function, which is declared in **string.h** (Chapter 6). You would not usually redefine a standard function unless you wanted to change its definition. That is legitimate C usage, as Exercise 5.36 demonstrates, but it is not usually a good idea to rewrite standard library functions. Exercise 5.36 uses the function to illustrate a valid usage for argument pointers to *const* variables.

---

const Pointer Variables

You can define pointers that cannot themselves change after they have been initialized. This practice allows you to build a small amount of safety into your code. If a pointer ought never be used to iterate—if it should always retain its original value—declare it as *const* in this way:

```
char * const ptr = buf;
```

This declaration builds a char pointer that is itself *const*. You can also have a *const* pointer as a function parameter. The function cannot modify the pointer itself. These measures let the compiler catch your errors. Exercise 5.37 shows *const* pointers.

EXERCISE 5.37 *const pointers.*

```
#include <stdio.h>
#include <ctype.h>

void ShowAllUppers(char * const str);

int main()
{
    char hb[] = "happy birthday";
    ShowAllUppers(hb);
    return 0;
}

void ShowAllUppers(char * const str)
{
    int i = 0;
    while (*(str+i))    {
        *(str+i) = toupper(*(str+i));
        i++;
    }
    puts(str);
}
```

Exercise 5.37 calls a function that converts a string constant to uppercase and then displays it. It uses the Standard C *toupper* function, which is declared in **ctype.h** (Chapter 6).

The function argument is a *const* pointer, which means that the function cannot change the value of the pointer. The reason, in this contrived example, is that the function needs the pointer's original value for the *puts* call after the conversion is done. The program would work the same if you removed the *const* qualification from the argument's declaration. If, however, you later modified the function to change the pointer, the compiler would not catch the error, and the *puts* call would be using the wrong value.

You declare a pointer that itself is *const* and that points to a *const* variable using this format:

```
const char * const ptr = buf;
```

void Pointers

A *void* pointer can point to any kind of variable. It is declared like this:

```
void *vptr;
```

You can assign any address to a *void* pointer. You cannot use a *void* pointer to dereference a variable unless you provide a *cast*, described in a later section. You cannot perform pointer arithmetic on a *void* pointer without a cast. You use *void* pointers as parameters to functions that can operate on any kind of memory. You return *void* pointers from functions to assign to any of several different kinds of pointers. Typical examples are the Standard C memory allocation functions declared in **stdlib.h** (Chapter 6). Exercise 5.38 declares the *malloc* and *free* function prototypes locally to show you how the *void* pointer mechanism works.

EXERCISE 5.38 *The* **void** *pointer.*

```
#include <stdio.h>
#include <stdlib.h>

void *malloc(int sz);    /* function returning void*        */
int free(void* bf);      /* function accepting void* argument */

struct Employee {        /* Employee record structure       */
    int emplno;
    char *name;
    float salary;
};

void ShowEmployee(struct Employee *emp);
```

continued

EXERCISE 5.38 *The void pointer (continued).*

```
int main()
{
    struct Employee *emp;
    emp = malloc(sizeof(struct Employee)); /* allocate memory */
    if (emp != NULL)    {
        /* --- build an Employee record --- */
        emp->emplno = 123;
        emp->name = "Jones";
        emp->salary = 37500;
        ShowEmployee(emp);
        free(emp);                    /* free allocated memory */
    }
    return 0;
}
/* ---- display an Employee record ---- */
void ShowEmployee(struct Employee *emp)
{
    printf("Empl#:  %d\nName:    %s\nSalary: %7.2f",
        emp->emplno, emp->name, emp->salary);
}
```

Exercise 5.38 calls *malloc* to allocate a block of memory big enough to hold an instance of an *Employee* structure. That call returns the address of a user-defined structure from a general-purpose memory allocation function. The function itself returns a *void* pointer, which is assigned to a pointer to the structure type. The function must return a *void* pointer, because you use the same memory allocation library functions to allocate memory for all types.

The program assigns some values to the structure members and calls a function to display the employee data. Then it calls the standard *free* function to release the memory that was allocated. The *free* function expects a *void* pointer to identify the memory to be freed. The program passes the address of a user-defined structure as an argument for the *void* pointer parameter. The *free* function declares a *void* pointer because it frees memory that was allocated for all types.

The *sizeof* Operator

Exercise 5.38 teaches another lesson. The program allocates 14 bytes of memory for the *Employee* structure by using the *sizeof* operator. This number works out to be 14 with Quincy because integers are two bytes long, pointers are four bytes, and a float is eight. The program could have used the constant 14 instead of the *sizeof* expression. There are three problems associated with this approach.

First, you have to count the bytes in a structure to know its size, and you could make a mistake. The *malloc* function wouldn't care; it allocates whatever you ask for. The assignment accepts whatever address *malloc* returns and assumes that there are enough bytes there to hold the structure.

The second problem arises when you change the size of the structure later during the program's development. Using an explicit constant size for the structure, you would have to find such references and change them.

The last problem is one of portability. The program would work only when the sizes of the intrinsic data types add up to 14. If you compiled the program with a different compiler or a different memory model or on a different computer, the sizes would probably be different, and the value 14 would be incorrect. The *sizeof* operator avoids all three of these problems.

The *sizeof* operator returns the size in characters of a variable or a type. The variable or type can be an array, structure, pointer, or one of the intrinsic types. When the operand is a type, such as the one in Exercise 5.38, the operand must be surrounded by parentheses. When the operand is a variable identifier, the parentheses are optional. Here are examples:

```
/* ----- some things to take the size of ----- */
int w;
int *x;
int y[5];
struct z { int a,b,c; };
struct z zs;
struct z *zp;
/* ----- some sizeof expressions ----- */
sizeof w;               /* the size of an int       */
sizeof(int);            /* the size of an int       */
sizeof x;               /* the size of a pointer    */
sizeof &w;              /* the size of a pointer    */
sizeof *x;              /* the size of an int       */
sizeof y;               /* the size of the array    */
sizeof(struct z);       /* the size of the structure */
sizeof zs;              /* the size of the structure */
sizeof zp;              /* the size of a pointer    */
```

Programs use *sizeof* as a portable way to express structure sizes and the sizes of input/output buffers.

You can also use *sizeof* to dynamically compute the number of elements in an array. Refer to the menu manager in Exercise 5.33. It uses three constants that you must modify when you add or delete selections in the menu. One constant identifies the last selection, which is always the Exit command. The next iterates through the menu. The third constant ensures that the user enters a valid menu selection. All three constants reflect the number of structure elements in the menu-defining array. By using *sizeof* to dynamically compute the number of elements, the program can automatically adjust to changes that you make to the menus. Exercise 5.39 shows how this works.

EXERCISE 5.39 *Using **sizeof** to compute array elements.*

```
const int Selections = sizeof menu / sizeof(struct mn);

main()
{
    /* ---- the menu manager ---- */
    unsigned i, sel = 0;
    while (sel != Selections)    {
        for (i = 0; i < Selections; i++)
            printf("\n%d: %s", i+1, menu[i].name);
        printf("\nSelect: ");
        scanf("%d", &sel);
        if (sel < Selections+1)
            /* --- call through function pointer --- */
            (*menu[sel-1].fn)();
    }
}
```

(The listing in Exercise 5.39 repeats only the changed parts of Exercise 5.33.) Exercise 5.39 defines a *const int* variable with an initialized value computed by dividing the size of the *menu* array by the size of one element—the *struct mn* type—in the array. The exercise uses the variable, *Selections*, instead of the constant expressions in Exercise 5.33. If you change the program later by adding or removing menu items or if you add members to the structure, the program adjusts to the new size, and the menu management code does not need to be modified.

Casts

Sometimes you need to coerce the compiler into thinking that a variable or constant is a different type from the one that you declared it to be or, as in the case of an expression, a different type than the one implied by its context. For that, you use a cast, which has this format:

```
int *iptr = (int*) &table;
```

The *(int*)* prefix to the expression is a cast. It tells the compiler to convert the value of the expression to the type in the cast. Some casts are not permitted. You cannot cast a structure of one type to something else. You can cast any numerical type to any other numerical type and any pointer to any other pointer. You can cast numerical values to pointers and vice versa, although such practices are generally considered unsafe and unnecessary.

Casts can be used to suppress compiler warnings. Some compilers warn you when an implicit type conversion could result in the loss of information. For example:

```
long el = 123;
int i = (int) el;  /* compiler warning without the cast */
```

Most compilers alert you that the assignment of a *long* to an *int* could lose data. There are times when you know better, as in the example. The value 123 is well within the range of an *int*. Other times you don't care, such as when you need the integral part of a real number:

```
float rn = 34.56;
int i = (int) rn;    /* i = 34 */
```

These are the best uses of the cast—to suppress compiler warnings about things that you do intentionally. Using the cast to override the compiler's limited type-checking facilities is a bad practice.

typedef

The C *typedef* storage class specifier does not really specify a storage class. It is grouped with the *static, extern, register,* and *auto* storage classes because all five appear syntactically in the same place in a declaration and because they are mutually exclusive. Therefore, *typedef* is called a storage class specifier. However, *typedef* has a much different role. It allows you to assign your own names to types, effectively building new types into your program. Exercise 5.40 is an example of *typedef*.

EXERCISE 5.40 *The **typedef** storage class.*

```
#include <stdio.h>

typedef int RcdCounter;

int main()
{
    RcdCounter rc = 123;
    printf("%d Records", rc);
    return 0;
}
```

Exercise 5.40 uses *typedef* to declare an integer type for a record counter. If you decide, later in the program's development, that a record counter needs to be a different integral type—*long*, perhaps, or *unsigned*—you can change the *typedef* declaration and the program adjusts all uses of it. Here are some of the ways that the *typedef* in Exercise 5.40 could be changed:

```
typedef long RcdCounter;
typedef unsigned RcdCounter;
typedef unsigned char RcdCounter;
```

You would have to modify related places that are type sensitive, such as the *printf* formatting string, but those instances are usually few.

The *typedef* storage class works with pointers and structures, too. Here is an example:

```
typedef struct window  {
    char *title;
    int x,y;
    int ht, wd;
} * WINDOW;
```

Pointers to the *window* structure can be declared with the *WINDOW* identifier. Perhaps the structure and *typedef* declarations are in a header file and the code that supports windows is in a library. Programmers don't even need to know that a *WINDOW* is a pointer or what it points to. The identifier is a *handle* used to communicate between the applications program and the screen manager library software, as in this example:

```
#include "windows.h"

void foo()
{
    WINDOW wnd = CreateWindow("hi", 3, 5, 10, 60);
    DisplayWindow(wnd);
    /* etc... */
}
```

The underlying structure of screen windows is unimportant to the programmer who uses the *WINDOW* handle. This practice is called *information hiding*, and it is a basic concept in structured programming.

Command Line Arguments: *argc* and *argv*

Every C program has a *main* function, a fact that you have been using in all the exercises in this book. The *main* function has two parameters that you have not yet seen because none of the programs have defined them. In fact, *main* is the only function that can get by without defining its parameters. The two parameters are an *int* and a pointer to an array of *char* pointers. The *int* parameter contains the number of command line arguments that the user typed on the command line to run the program. The *char* []* argument points to an array of character pointers, which themselves point to the command line arguments. Although you may name these two parameters anything you like, the convention is to name them *argc* and *argv* and to declare them in the *main* function header this way:

```
int main(int argc, char *argv[])
{
    /* ... */
}
```

The *argc* parameter has at least a count of 1 and more if the user keyed command line arguments. There is always at least one *char* pointer in the array pointed to by *argv*, and it, *argv[0]*, usually points to the name of the program's executable file. Some implementations include the path that the program is run from. Most MS-DOS implementations work that way. Figure 5.4 shows a program named EZAcct that has four command line arguments.

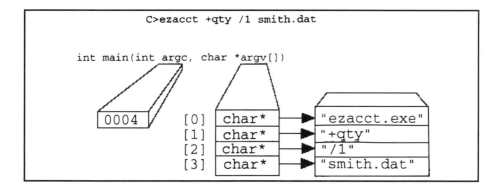

FIGURE 5.4 *Command line arguments.*

 NOTE

Quincy is a C interpreter that does not produce executable files. Therefore, although you run Quincy from the command line, you do not run your C programs from the command line. Instead, you run them from within Quincy's integrated development environment. Quincy emulates command line entries, however, and some of the exercises take advantage of that. Before proceeding, you should refer again to the Appendix and refresh your knowledge of how to set command line arguments into Quincy's operating environment.

Exercise 5.41 shows how a program uses command line arguments.

EXERCISE 5.41 *Command line arguments.*

```
#include <stdio.h>

int main(int argc, char *argv[])
{
    int arg;
    printf("This program is %s", argv[0]);
    for (arg = 1; arg < argc; arg++)
        printf("\narg %d: %s", arg, argv[arg]);
}
```

Summary

With the exercises and lessons in this chapter, you learned about the scope of identifiers, storage classes, type qualifiers, structures, unions, enumerated data types, arrays, pointers, addresses, the *sizeof* operator, casts, *typedefs*, and command line arguments.

Chapter 6

LIBRARY FUNCTIONS

Standard C includes a full library of portable functions. You have used some of them in the exercises in earlier chapters. Quincy does not implement the complete Standard C library, and this book does not teach them all. There are no technical reasons that prevent Quincy from including every function in the standard. Rather, they are selected from the ones that should be the most useful to new C programmers and that best teach the language and its software development environment.

This chapter is organized alphabetically by the header files where library functions are declared. To use a function from the standard library, you must include its header file in your program ahead of any references to the function. Some of the standard header files define global values, macros, functions, and data structures that support the library and your use of it.

A *macro* looks like a function, or in some cases a macro assigns an identifier to a value. You learn how to build your own macros by using the *#define* pre-processor directive discussed in Chapter 8.

This chapter describes many of the functions and macros without detailed examples. You have already used some of them, and many of them are similar enough that you do not need anything more than a description. However, where examples provide better explanations, the chapter includes exercises. You will learn about the functions in:

▼ **Assert.h**

▼ **Ctype.h**

▼ **Errno.h**

▼ **Math.h**

▼ **Setjmp.h**

▼ **Stdarg.h**

▼ **Stdio.h**

▼ **Stdlib.h**

▼ **String.h**

▼ **Time.h**

Assert.h

The **assert.h** header is for debugging. It defines the *assert* macro, which lets the compiler help you debug the program with defensive code.

There are certain program conditions that you assume to be just so. You intend for them to be so and expect the code to run as if they are so. If the conditions are not as you assume them to be, a program bug results. You could put tests throughout your program for these conditions, but, since you fully intend for them to be a certain way, you do not want the distributed program to bear the burden of code that serves only to ensure that the program works the way you intended.

You can have your validation code during testing and remove it for the production program without a lot of fuss. The *assert* macro asserts that a condition is true. If it is not, the macro displays the condition and where in the program the test failed and aborts the program.

When the program is completely checked out and none of the assertions fail, you can disable the tests by defining the *NDEBUG* macro and doing a final compile. The *NDEBUG* macro changes all *assert* macro calls to null expressions. Exercise 6.1 demonstrates the use of the *assert* macro.

EXERCISE 6.1 *The assert macro.*

```
#include <stdio.h>
#include <assert.h>

void DisplayMsg(char *msg);

int main()
{
    char *cp = NULL;
    DisplayMsg(cp);
    return 0;
}

void DisplayMsg(char *msg)
{
    assert(msg != NULL);
    puts(msg);
}
```

Exercise 6.1 has a bug, which the *assert* macro catches. The *main* function calls the *DisplayMsg* function with a NULL pointer argument. When you run this program, the *assert* macro displays the following message and aborts the program:

```
assert failed: (msg != NULL) File: ex06001.c, Line: 25
```

The message tells you that the *assert* call on line 16 of the translation unit named **ex06001.c** failed. It even displays the condition that was false and that caused the abort.

When you use the *assert* macro, you are asserting that a condition must be true. It is a good practice to use *assert* in places where your program makes assumptions about values and other conditions.

You can correct the program by passing a valid pointer to *DisplayMsg*. Then you can insert this line of code ahead of the code that includes **assert.h**:

```
#define NDEBUG
```

It is better to use this technique than to take out all the *assert* calls. Leave them in. They'll be there to help you debug the program when you make modifications to it later.

Ctype.h

The functions in **ctype.h** convert *char* variables and test them for defined ranges. You used the *toupper* function in Exercise 5.37.

Some C implementations, Quincy included, implement the **ctype.h** functions as macros. Table 6.1 summarizes the *ctype* functions.

TABLE 6.1 *Ctype.h functions/macros.*

CTYPE.H FUNCTION/MACRO	RETURNS:
int isdigit(int c);	true if c is a digit (0-9)
int isupper(int c);	true if c is an uppercase letter (A-Z)
int islower(int c);	true if c is a lowercase letter (a-z)
int isalpha(int c);	true if c is an alphabetic character (A-Z,a-z)
int isalnum(int c);	true if isalpha(c) or isdigit(c)
int isprint(int c);	true if c is a displayable ASCII character
int isspace(int c);	true if c is a white space character
int toupper(int c);	the uppercase equivalent of c
int tolower(int c);	the lowercase equivalent of c

Do not use expressions that could have side effects when you call macros in **ctype.h**. Depending on how the macro is implemented, the side effects could produce incorrect results. This statement, for example, has potential side effects:

```
a = toupper(c++);
```

A side effect is an action that changes the value of a variable in an argument or an argument that uses a function call in its expression. The auto-increment operator changes the variable argument. The expansion of the macro could cause the argument expression to be evaluated more than once. The variable would be incremented more than once, which is a hidden side effect of the macro.

You will learn about side effects in Chapter 8.

Errno.h

The **errno.h** header defines a global modifiable *lvalue* named *errno* and global symbols named *EDOM* and *ERANGE*.

Some library functions set a value into *errno* to indicate that an error occurred in a function call. The ANSI Standard defines only the two error values *EDOM*, which means that an error occurred in an argument to a math function, and *ERANGE*, which means that a floating point number is too big.

The value of *errno* is zero when the program starts. If a library function sets it to some value, it retains that value until something changes it. Therefore, if you are going to use *errno* after a function call, set it to zero before the function call. Exercise 6.2 demonstrates the use of *errno*.

EXERCISE 6.2 *Using errno.*

```
#include <stdio.h>
#include <math.h>
#include <errno.h>

int main()
{
    double f = 1, sq;
    while(f != 0)    {
        errno = 0;
        printf("\nEnter float (0 to quit) ");
        scanf("%f", &f);
        sq = sqrt(f);
        if (errno == 0)
            printf("Square root of %f is %f", f, sq);
    }
}
```

Exercise 6.2 uses the *sqrt* function from **math.h**, discussed next, to compute the square root of a number entered by the user. If, for example, you enter a negative number or a number too big to be held in a *double*, the function sets *errno* to a nonzero value. The program displays the square root only if there is no error indicated by *errno*.

Math.h

The **math.h** header declares the standard math functions. You just used one of them, *sqrt*, in Exercise 6.2. Table 6.2 summarizes the others.

TABLE 6.2 *Math.h functions.*

MATH.H FUNCTION	RETURNS
double acos(double x);	arc cosine of x
double asin(double x);	arc sine of x
double atan(double x);	arc tangent of x
double atan2(double y,double x);	arc tangent of y/x
double ceil(double x);	smallest integer not < x
double cos(double x);	cosine of x
double cosh(double x);	hyperbolic cosine of x
double exp(double x);	exponential value of x
double fabs(double x);	absolute value of x
double floor(double x);	largest integer not > x
double log(double x);	natural logarithm of x
double log10(double x);	base-10 logarithm of x
double pow(double x,double y);	x raised to the power y
double sin(double x);	sin of x
double sinh(double x);	hyberbolic sine of x
double sqrt(double x);	square root of x
double tan(double x);	tangent of x
double tanh(double x);	hyperbolic tangent of x

Setjmp.h

The **setjmp.h** header defines two functions—*setjmp* and *longjmp*—and a data type, the *jmp_buf* structure.

The functions in **setjmp.h** are used to jump from somewhere in the depths of the called functions to a defined place higher in the program. Why would you want to do that? One example is a program that validates records in an input stream. The program might detect an error in a function that is deep into the function calling stack. This is particularly true if the program uses recursive descent parsing logic. The program needs to reject the data in question and return to the top of the program to read the next record.

One approach is to set an error variable and return. Every function tests the error variable upon return from every lower function call and returns to its caller rather than proceeding with the current input record. This approach is error-prone and uses additional code to manage and test the error variable.

C provides *setjmp* and *longjmp* to serve this purpose. The *setjmp* function records the program's operating state in a *jmp_buf* structure. A *longjmp* call from a lower function can reference the *jmp_buf* structure and cause an immediate jump to the place where the matching *setjmp* occurred.

Remember the calculator program in Exercise 4.14. When it found an input error, it aborted the program. Exercise 6.3 modifies that program to use *setjmp* and *longjmp* to keep the program running after an error is found.

The listings shown here include the modified *main* and *error* functions, the *#include <setjmp.h>* statement, and the definition of the *jmp_buf* variable. The rest of the program is the same as Exercise 4.14.

EXERCISE 6.3 *setjmp and longjmp.*

```
#include <setjmp.h>

/* --- error jmp_buf buffer --- */
jmp_buf errjb;

int main()
{
    int ans = -1;
    while (ans != 0)    {
        /* --- mark the top of the parsing descent --- */
        if (setjmp(errjb) == 0) {
            pos = 0;    /* initialize string subscript */
            /* ---- read an expression ----- */
            puts("\nEnter expression (0 to quit): ");
            gets(expr);
```

continued

Exercise 6.3 *setjmp* and *longjmp* (continued).

```
                /* --- evaluate the expression --- */
                ans = addsubt();
                if (expr[pos] != '\0')
                    error();
                printf("%d", ans);
            }
        else
            /* --- an error occurred --- */
            printf("\nTry again");
    }
    return 0;
}
```

```
/* ---- syntax error ---- */
void error(void)
{
    putchar('\r');
    while (pos--)            /* position error pointer */
        putchar(' ');
    printf("^ syntax error");
    longjmp(errjb, 1);  /* return to top of program */
}
```

The *setjmp* function marks the program's position and context and stores that information in its *jmp_buf* argument. Then *setjmp* returns zero. The *longjmp* function restores the program's context from its *jmp_buf* argument and jumps to the associated *setjmp* expression, causing the *setjmp* call to return the value of the *longjmp* call's second argument. If Exercise 6.3 senses an error in the user's expression entry, it jumps to the *main* function at the point of the *setjmp* call, returning the value 1. The *error* function invocation that reports the error could be several levels down in the recursive descent parsing algorithm, but the *longjmp* call restores the program's function depth context to the top of the program.

Stdarg.h

Recall from Chapter 3 that functions with variable parameter lists are declared with ellipses such as this:

```
void DoList(int, ...);
```

Several of the functions declared in **stdio.h**, discussed next, use ellipses. It is the mechanism by which calls to the standard *printf* function can pass any kind and number of arguments after the formatting string. The ellipses tell the compiler not to check parameter types in calls to the function. In this example, the compiler ensures that the first argument is an *int*; it ignores the rest of the arguments.

You write a function that has variable arguments by including **stdarg.h** and using a *typedef* and the three macros defined there. The *typedef* defines the *va_list* type. The macros are *va_start*, *va_arg*, and *va_end*. Exercise 6.4 shows how these macros are used.

Exercise 6.4 *Variable argument lists.*

```
#include <stdio.h>
#include <stdarg.h>

void Presidents(int n, ...)
{
    va_list ap;
    va_start(ap, n);
    while (n--) {
        char *nm = va_arg(ap, char *);   /* char* argument */
        int year = va_arg(ap, int);      /* int argument   */
        printf("\n%d %s", year, nm);
    }
    va_end(ap);
}

int main()
{
    Presidents(4, "Carter", 1976, "Reagan", 1980,
                  "Bush", 1988, "Clinton", 1992);
    return 0;
}
```

A function with variable arguments usually needs at least one fixed argument that it can use to determine the number and types of the other arguments. For example, the formatting string tells *printf* what follows. Exercise 6.4 takes an integer first argument as a count of the pairs of arguments that follow. Then it assumes that the list has that many argument pairs of one character pointer and one integer.

va_list

The macros use the *va_list* variable as a point of reference.

va_start

Scanning the variable argument list starts with the *va_start* macro call which takes the names of the *va_list* variable and the function's fixed argument as macro arguments. The *va_start* macro establishes the starting point for the variable argument scan and stores that information in the *va_list* variable. If the function had more than one fixed argument, the *va_start* macro would use the identifier of the last one immediately before the ellipse.

va_arg

The function uses the *va_arg* macro to extract arguments from the variable argument list. The *va_arg* macro's arguments are the *va_list* variable and the type of the next expected argument. Observe that the two *va_arg* macro calls have *int* and *char** as their second argument. The function knows what types of arguments to expect. It knows how many based on the value stored in the fixed argument.

va_end

The *va_end* macro takes the *va_list* variable as an argument. In many C language implementations, Quincy included, this macro does nothing. You should always include it, though, so that your programs are portable to other compilers and other computers.

Because the compiler does no type checking of arguments represented by the ellipse in function declarations, you can pass anything at all to a variable-argument function. Naturally, if you pass something other than what the function expects, the results are unpredictable.

Stdio.h

The **stdio.h** header declares functions and global symbols that support standard input and output. C programs use standard devices for all input and output. Unless you redirect them, the standard input device is the keyboard, and the standard output device is the screen. There are also standard print, error, and auxiliary devices. Chapter 7 discusses all the standard devices and explains how you can redirect standard input and output to disk files.

Global Symbols

Stdio.h declares several global symbols with *typedef* statements and *#define* (Chapter 8) macros. Most of these have to do with disk files, which Chapter 7 discusses. Curiously, **stdio.h** defines *NULL*, the global symbol that represents a null pointer. *NULL* has nothing to do with standard input/output except that some of the functions return a null pointer. **Stdio.h** defines it by tradition.

Standard Input/Output Functions

Most of the exercises in this and earlier chapters use **stdio.h** functions to read the keyboard and write to the screen. You learned about *puts, putchar, getchar, printf,* and *scanf* in Chapter 2. Table 6.3 lists the standard input/output functions in **stdio.h**, most of which you have already seen.

TABLE 6.3 *Stdio.h console functions.*

```
int getchar(void);
int putchar(int c);
int printf(const char *fmt, ...);
int scanf(const char *fmt, ...);
char *gets(char *s);
int puts(const char *s);
```

Table 6.3 includes *gets* (pronounced *get-ess*), a function that you haven't seen yet. It reads a string of characters from the standard input device and stores them in the buffer pointed to by the function's argument. The function reads characters from standard input until it sees a *newline* character or reaches end of file. It does not store the *newline* or EOF character in the buffer, and it terminates the buffer with a null character ('\0').

The *gets* function is not always safe to use. It assumes that the buffer pointed to by its argument has enough room to hold all the characters that are read. You cannot control how many keys the user presses. Most programmers prefer to use *fgets* (Chapter 7) to read strings from standard input.

String Formatting Functions

Stdio.h declares two string formatting functions that resemble *printf* and *scanf* but that use memory buffers rather than input/output devices. Table 6.4 lists them.

TABLE 6.4 *Stdio.h string formatting functions.*

```
int sprintf(char *s,const char *fmt, ...);
int sscanf(char *s, const char *fmt, ...);
```

The *sprintf* function works just like *printf* except that its output is written to the memory address pointed to by its first argument rather than to standard output. The function assumes that the memory buffer is big enough to hold the entire formatted string, including a null terminator, which the function adds.

The *sscanf* function works just like *scanf* except that it takes its input from the memory address pointed to by its first argument rather than from standard input.

Stdio.h declares several more functions related to file input/output. Chapter 7 discusses them.

Stdlib.h

Stdlib.h declares a number of standard library functions and macros in four categories: numerical functions, memory allocation functions, system functions, and random number generation.

Numerical Functions

Table 6.5 lists the **stdlib.h** numerical functions and what each one returns.

TABLE 6.5 *Stdlib.h* numerical functions.

STDLIB.H NUMERICAL FUNCTION	RETURNS
int abs(int i);	the absolute value of i
int atoi(const char *s);	the integer value of the string
long atol(const char *s);	the long integer value of the string
float atof(const char *s);	the float value of the string

Memory Allocation Functions

C programs have a store of memory available for dynamic allocations. That store is called the *heap*. A program can allocate memory from the heap and return the memory to the heap when the program is finished using it. Dynamic memory allocation allows a program to use memory buffers only when they are needed. That way a program can operate in a system with an amount of available memory smaller than the program's total requirement. Table 6.6 lists the memory allocation functions.

TABLE 6.6 *Stdlib.h* memory allocation functions.

STDLIB.H MEMORY ALLOCATION FUNCTION	RETURNS
void *calloc(int sz, int n);	address of buffer or NULL
void *malloc(int sz);	address of buffer or NULL
void free(void *buf);	nothing

You used *malloc* and *free* in Exercise 5.38. The *calloc* function is similar to *malloc* with these exceptions. First, instead of specifying a character count for the memory allocation, you specify an item size and the number of items. Second, *calloc* initializes the allocated memory to zeros, whereas *malloc* does not.

If there is not enough memory available for either *malloc* or *calloc*, they return NULL. Programs should always check for a NULL return and do something appropriate when that happens. Ignoring a NULL return could crash the system when the program tries to assign values through a NULL pointer.

System Functions

Stdlib.h declares functions related to the operation of the program as shown in Table 6.7.

TABLE 6.7 *Stdlib.h* system functions.

```
void abort(void);
void exit(int n);
int system(const char *cmd);
```

The *abort* and *exit* functions terminate the program. The *abort* function is used for an abnormal termination. It returns –1 to the operating system in the Quincy implementation. Standard C does not define a value for *abort* to return except to specify that it returns an implementation-dependent *unsuccessful termination* value. The *exit* function is for normal termination. It closes all open stream files and returns to the operating system whatever value you pass as an argument.

The *system* function calls the operating system to execute an operating system command. In MS-DOS, the commands executed are the same as commands you would type on the DOS command line. Exercise 6.5 demonstrates the *system* function by executing the DOS *dir* command to view a list of Quincy's header files.

EXERCISE 6.5 *The system* function.

```
#include <stdlib.h>

int main()
{
    system("dir *.h");
}
```

Random Number Generation Functions

Exercises 4.8, 4.9, 4.11, and 4.12 used the *rand* and *srand* functions shown in Table 6.8 to compute random numbers.

TABLE 6.8 *Stdlib.h random number functions.*

> nt rand(void);
>
> void srand(unsigned int seed);

Recall that Exercise 4.8 is a guessing game. The program computes a random number and you guess what it is. The problem with that program is that the random number generator is predictable. It always starts with the same number and progresses through an identical sequence of numbers, which isn't random at all. Exercise 6.6 adds one line of code to the program to make the first random number less predictable. It calls *srand* to seed the generator with a value based on the current date and time. The *time* function, described later in this chapter, returns an integer value based on the system clock. That value is the seed in Exercise 6.6.

EXERCISE 6.6 *Seeding the random number generator.*

```c
#include <stdio.h>
#include <stdlib.h>
#include <time.h>

int main()
{
    char ans;
    srand(time(NULL));
    /* --- loop until user is done --- */
    do  {
        int num;
        int fav = rand() % 32;  /* choose a secret number */
        /* --- loop until user guesses secret number --- */
        do  {
            printf("Guess my secret number (0 - 32) ");
            scanf("%d", &num);
            /* --- report the status of the guess --- */
            puts(num < fav ? "Too low"  :
                 num > fav ? "Too high" :
                             "Right");
        } while (num != fav);
        printf("Go again? (y/n) ");
        scanf("%c", &ans);
    } while (ans == 'y');
    return 0;
}
```

String.h

The **string.h** header declares functions that work with null-terminated character arrays. There are two comparison functions, two copy functions, two concatenation functions, one function to return the length of a string, and one function to fill an area of memory with a specified character value. Table 6.9 lists the **string.h** functions.

TABLE 6.9 *String.h functions.*

```
int strcmp(const char *s1, const char *s2);
int strncmp(const char *s1, const char *s2, int n);
char *strcpy(char *s1, const char *s2);
char *strncpy(char *s1, const char *s2, int n);
int strlen(const char *s);
char *strcat(char *s1, const char *s2);
char *strncat(char *s1, const char *s2, int n);
char *memset(void *s, int c, int n)
```

Exercise 6.7 demonstrates the *strcmp*, *strcpy*, and *strlen* functions.

EXERCISE 6.7 *strcmp, strcpy, and strlen.*

```c
#include <stdio.h>
#include <string.h>

int main()
{
    char pwd[40];
    int len;
    char msg[] = "Wrong";

    puts("Password?");
    gets(pwd);
    /* --- find string length --- */
    len = strlen(pwd);
```

continued

EXERCISE 6.7 *strcmp, strcpy, and strlen (continued).*

```
    /* --- compare string with string constant --- */
    if (strcmp(pwd, "boobah") == 0)
        /* --- copy constant to message --- */
        strcpy(msg, "OK");
    printf("%s. You typed %d characters", msg, len);
    return 0;
}
```

You run the program in Exercise 6.7 and enter a password in response to the prompt. Do not enter more than 39 characters or you will overwrite the 40-character *pwd* array.

strlen

The program passes the address of the password to *strlen* to get the length of the input string, which counts all the characters except the null terminator.

strcmp

The *strcmp* function compares two strings. It returns zero if the two strings are equal, less than zero if the first string is less than the second string, and greater than zero if the first string is greater than the second string. Comparisons proceed from the first character in both strings and iterate forward until null terminators are found or different character values are found in the strings. If one string is shorter than the other and all of the character values are equal up to the end of the shorter string, the longer string compares greater than the shorter one.

strcpy

If the password you typed is equal to the constant password, the program calls *strcpy* to copy the string constant "OK" to the *msg* string. This operation over-writes the *msg* string's initialized value of "Wrong". The *msg* array has six elements based on the default dimension declared by its initializer. The *strcpy* function copies only three characters: 'O', 'K', and a null terminator. The result-ing *msg* array looks like this in memory:

```
'O', 'K', '\0', 'n', 'g', '\0'
```

If the second string argument to *strcpy* is longer than five characters plus a null terminator, the results are unpredictable. Usually, the program fails immediately or soon afterward because it has overwritten whatever coincidentally follows the receiving array in memory.

strcat

The *strcat* function appends the string value of its second argument to the string in its first argument. There must be enough space past the significant characters (up to the null terminator) of the first argument for the second argument and its null terminator. For example:

```
char s[13] = "Hello";  /* must be at least 13 chars */
strcat(s, ", Dolly");  /* s1 = "Hello, Dolly"        */
```

strncmp, strncpy, and strncat

These three functions are similar to the three functions above except that each has a third integer parameter that specifies the maximum number of characters to compare, copy, or concatenate. If the second argument to *strncpy* has fewer characters to copy than the integer argument specifies, the function pads the remaining characters in the first argument with zeros.

memset

The *memset* function is not just a string function. It fills a block of memory with a specified character. Its first argument is a void pointer to the block of memory. By using a void pointer in its declaration, the function allows you to use it to initialize any buffer. The second argument specifies the fill character value. The third argument specifies the length of the memory area to be filled. The *memset* function is most often used to zero-fill uninitialized memory for data aggregates such as structures and arrays.

Time.h

Time.h declares several functions, a structure, and a data type related to time and date. The structure is shown here:

```
struct tm
{
   int   tm_sec;    /* seconds (0-61)              */
   int   tm_min;    /* minutes (0-59)              */
   int   tm_hour;   /* hours   (0-23               */
   int   tm_mday;   /* day of the month (1-31)     */
   int   tm_mon;    /* months since January (0-11) */
   int   tm_year;   /* years since 1900            */
   int   tm_wday;   /* days since Sunday (0-6)     */
   int   tm_yday;   /* days since January 1 (0-365) */
   int   tm_isdst;  /* Daylight Savings Time flag  */
};
```

The data type is *typedef long time_t*. It is an integer value that represents the date and time as the number of clock ticks since a defined time in the past. Applications programs do not deal with the actual integral representation of the time. Instead, they accept and pass *time_t* values between functions declared in **time.h**.

Table 6.10 lists the time and date functions.

TABLE 6.10 *Time.h functions.*

```
char *asctime(const struct tm *tim);
char *ctime(const time_t *t);
double difftime(time_t t1, time_t t2);
struct tm *gmtime(const time_t *t);
struct tm *localtime(const time_t *t);
time_t mktime(struct tm *tim);
time_t time(time_t *t);
```

asctime

This function converts the *struct tm* structure pointed to by its argument into a null-terminated string suitable for displaying. The string is in this format:

```
"Mon Apr 25 14:41:22 1994\n"
```

ctime

This function converts the *time_t* variable pointed to by its argument into a string in the same format as the string produced by *asctime*.

difftime

This function returns a *double* value representing the difference in seconds between its two *time_t* arguments by subtracting the second argument from the first.

gmtime

This function converts the *time_t* variable pointed to by its argument into a *struct tm* variable representing Coordinated Universal Time, which is also called Greenwich mean time. It returns a pointer to the structure that it builds.

localtime

This function converts the *time_t* variable pointed to by its argument into a *struct tm* variable representing local time. It returns a pointer to the structure that it builds.

mktime

This function converts the *struct tm* variable pointed to by its argument into a *time_t* variable, which *mktime* returns.

time

This function returns the current time as a *time_t* variable. If its argument is not NULL, the function also copies the *time_t* variable into the variable pointed to by the argument.

Exercise 6.8 uses some of the functions here to display the current Greenwich mean time.

EXERCISE 6.8 *Time.h functions.*

```
#include <stdio.h>
#include <time.h>

int main()
{
    time_t now = time(NULL);
    printf("%s", asctime(gmtime(&now)));
    return 0;
}
```

Summary

This chapter discussed the Standard C library functions that Quincy implements. The Quincy library subset is sufficient to teach the use of standard libraries and to write significant programs. When you begin using other compiler systems, you will find that they offer not only the standard library but also many other compiler-dependent libraries. You can also use third-party libraries that support different functional applications and operating environments. There are libraries for graphics, user interfaces, database management, communications, mathematics, direct access to DOS functions, and many more.

Chapter 7

FILES

*7*he exercises in previous chapters have dealt exclusively with console input/output. Programs of consequence, however, use not only the console but also disk files. In this chapter I teach you about the standard library functions that support creating, accessing, modifying, and deleting disk files. Those functions and data structures to support them are declared in the **stdio.h** header file.

Standard I/O Devices

Files are either streams of characters or records of binary data. A C program opens files, reads and writes data, and closes the files when the program is finished with them. The system console consists of two character stream files. The system maintains them as perpetually open files among Standard C's standard input/output devices. Programs read the keyboard by reading the *standard input* device and write to the screen by writing the *standard output* and *standard error* devices. In some C implementations, the printer is the *standard print* device, although the ANSI standard does not define it. All these standard devices are accessed as sequential character stream files in C.

Quincy's **stdio.h** header file defines five global constants that represent the five standard devices supported by MS-DOS systems. Table 7.1 lists those device identifier constants.

TABLE 7.1 *Standard MS-DOS input/output devices.*

DEVICE IDENTIFIER	DEVICE USE	DEVICE
stdin	Input	CON: (unless redirected)
stdout	Output	CON: (unless redirected)
stderr	Error	CON:
stdaux	Auxiliary	COM1:
stdprn	Printer	PRN:

The standard device identifiers are actually FILE pointers. Programs use them to address the standard devices. The FILE data type is defined with a *typedef* in **stdio.h**. Programs use them to identify files. The system provides a FILE pointer when you open a file, and you use that pointer in all function calls related to the open file. The five FILE pointers in Table 7.1 are predefined by the system to represent their respective standard devices. Others are created dynamically when you open files.

Standard input and output are the keyboard and screen by default, but they can be redirected to files. Standard error is the screen regardless of the redirection of standard output. Standard auxiliary is the communications device. Standard printer is the printer.

These standard devices are accessed in *text* mode. Programs read and write them sequentially in the order that the characters appear in the file. Disk files can be either text or *binary* mode, and programs can access their data in random sequence.

Most console input/output operations use the functions discussed in Chapter 6 under the heading "**Stdio.h**." Those functions use *stdin* and *stdout* by default. Other functions address files by using a FILE pointer. Those file functions are declared in **stdio.h**, too.

Input/Output Redirection

The simplest way to read and write files is to redirect standard input and output to disk files. I/O redirection tells the system to substitute disk files for the keyboard or the screen or both. Redirected standard input comes from a text file with ASCII data in the file just as you would type it on the keyboard. It could be prepared with a text editor or created by the standard output of another program. Redirected standard output is written to a text file with data that would have been displayed on the screen if standard output had not been redirected. Exercise 7.1 reads a text file and converts tabs in the text to spaces with tab stops every four character positions.

Exercise 7.1 *Redirecting **stdin** and **stdout**.*

```
#include <stdio.h>

int main()
{
    int c, x = 0;
    while ((c = getchar()) != EOF)  {
        if (c == '\t')  {
            do
                putchar(' ');
            while ((++x % 4) != 0);
            continue;
        }
        if (c == '\n')
            x = 0;
        putchar(c);
        x++;
    }
}
```

The program in Exercise 7.1 reads standard input until it reads the *EOF* character, which signifies end-of-file in stream files. *EOF* is a global constant defined as a macro in **stdio.h**. The program copies standard input to standard output, inserting spaces where it finds tab characters. Spaces are inserted to position each tab stop at intervals of four character positions.

If you run Exercise 7.1 without redirecting standard input, you must enter its input from the keyboard ending with a **Ctrl+Z** for the EOF character. You redirect standard input on the command line when you run the program like this as shown in the following example. Note that there is no file named **test.dat** among the exercises. This example gives the format for input redirection.

```
< test.dat
```

From the DOS command line, the redirection option just shown comes after the program name. It can come before or after any other command line options including redirection of standard output, described next. The "less-than" character tells DOS to redirect the named file into the program through standard input. The program reads characters from this file instead of the keyboard, and the system passes the program the EOF character when it senses end-of-file.

NOTE This is a good time to refer again to the Quincy User's Manual in the Appendix for instructions on how to add command line parameters and input/output redirection to Quincy programs.

One way to run Exercise 7.1 is to let it convert the tab characters in one of the exercise source files, perhaps even its own. You can view the output on the screen or redirect standard output to a file. Be aware that this action replaces an existing file with the same name.

To redirect standard output to a file, use the "greater-than" character and a file name on the command line:

```
> test.new
```

From the DOS command line, the redirection option just shown comes after the program name. It can come before or after any other command line options, including redirection of standard input. By now you know how to read and write the console well enough. From this point on in this chapter, we focus exclusively on disk files.

Opening Files

Before you can read or write a disk file, you must open it. Before you can open an existing file, it must have been created. Sometimes a program requires that a file already exists. Other times the file can be created if it doesn't exist and used if it does. These conditions are controlled by the standard library *fopen* function.

fopen

You create new disk files and open existing disk files by calling *fopen*:

```
FILE *fopen(const char *filename, const char *mode);
```

The *filename* argument is a null-terminated character string containing a file name that conforms to the file-naming conventions of the operating system. MS-DOS file names consist of up to eight characters, a dot, and a file extension of up to three characters. The *filename* can include a path prefix with a drive letter and subdirectories. If you don't include a path, the program searches for or creates the file in the current subdirectory.

The *mode* argument points to a string that specifies whether the file is to be created, whether it is to be read, written, or both, and whether the program wishes to access the data in text or binary mode. Table 7.2 summarizes the valid mode argument values.

TABLE 7.2 *fopen mode argument values.*

MODE	FORMAT	ACCESS	FILE CONDITION
"r"	Text	Read	Must exist
"w"	Text	Write	Create or replace
"a"	Text	Append	Create or open at end-of-file
"rb"	Binary	Read	Must exist
"wb"	Binary	Write	Create or replace
"ab"	Binary	Append	Create or open at end-of-file
"r+"	Text	Update	Must exist
"w+"	Text	Update	Create or replace
"a+"	Text	Update	Create or open at end-of-file
"r+b" or "rb+"	Binary	Update	Must exist
"w+b" or "wb+"	Binary	Update	Create or replace
"a+b" or "ab+"	Binary	Update	Create or open at end-of-file

Here is an example of a call to *fopen*:

```
FILE *fp = fopen("c:\\personel\\employee.dat", "r");
```

In this example the file name argument contains a complete MS-DOS file specification: drive, directories, and file name.

N O T E

Observe the double backslash character pairs in the string constant. You will remember from Chapter 2 that string constants can contain escape sequences that begin with a backslash. A double backslash is the escape sequence that puts a backslash in the constant, and MS-DOS uses the backslash character to separate drives, subdirectory specifications, and file names in a file path.

File Access Mode

The first character of the mode argument string is "r," "w," or "a," for *read*, *write*, or *append* access.

A file opened with read access must exist. The function fails (returns NULL) if no file exists having the file name specified in the first argument.

A file opened with write access is created if it does not exist and replaced if it does.

A file opened with append access is created if it does not exist; if it does exist, it is opened with write access starting at the end of the file.

The second character (and sometimes the third—see below) of the mode argument can be a "+" specifying that the file is opened in *update* mode, which means that the program can read and write the file. For read-update mode ("r+"), the file must exist. For write-update mode ("w+"), the file is created or replaced. For append-update mode ("a+"), the file is created or appended. Input and output operations must be separated by file-positioning actions (*fseek* or *rewind* calls) except that you can write to a file immediately following a read operation that reached end-of-file.

Text and Binary Files

The second character (or third if "+" is in the second position) of the mode argument can be a "b" specifying that the file is to be accessed in binary rather than the default text mode. Some C implementations allow you to use a "t" in this position to indicate text mode, although this usage is redundant and undefined by the ANSI standard.

Text Mode

Text mode is the default. Lines of text in a C program are null-terminated character arrays with a *newline* ("\n") character in the last position. Programs use the newline character in output streams to emulate the action of the carriage return key on a typewriter, which advances the current character position one line down and to the left margin. These two actions are represented in a text file with two characters: the carriage return (0x0d) and line feed (0x0a) characters. When a program writes a newline character to a file in text mode, the system translates that character into the carriage return, line feed pair. When a program reads text from a file in text mode, the system translates a carriage return, line feed pair into a single newline character.

The newline character has the same hexadecimal configuration as the line feed character. The carriage return character can be represented with a constant escape sequence ("\r"), too. The relationship between text data in memory and files is shown by Figure 7.1.

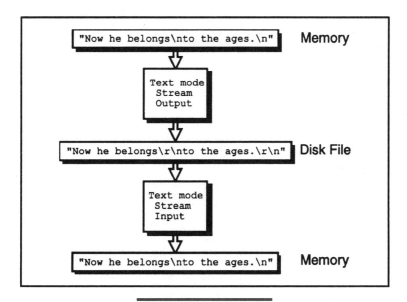

Figure 7.1 *Text mode input/output.*

Observe that there are more characters in the file than are in memory. The added "\r" characters account for the difference.

BINARY MODE

Text files contain variable-length text data. Binary files contain fixed or variable-length formatted data records. Newline conversion of binary data would create problems. A byte with a binary configuration matching the newline character would be converted as if it were a newline, which it probably is not. It might instead be part (or all) of an integer value. You want to read it into memory and write it to the file without translation. You should always open non-text files in binary mode.

The *fopen* Return Value

The *fopen* function returns the address of a FILE variable. This address is the handle that the program uses to reference the open file in subsequent standard file function calls. If the system cannot open the file in the manner requested, *fopen* returns NULL.

You should always test the return value from *fopen* to determine whether the open was successful. Unsuccessful opens occur when a file opened for read access does not exist, when a file opened for write, append, or update access is write-protected, when the file system is out of disk space, because of protection violations, or because of any of a number of platform-dependent exceptional conditions that prevent the program from opening the file.

Closing Files

When your program is finished accessing a file, it should close the file. Closing a file flushes its output buffer and releases the internal file system handle that represents the open file. Operating systems typically have a limited number of handles that programs can have open at any one time. You should close unneeded files to make the handles available for other use.

If the program does not close all of its open files, the system closes them when the program terminates. All ANSI-conforming C implementations do this when the *main* function returns or when the program calls the **stdlib.h** *exit* function. They do not necessarily close open files when the program calls the *abort* function, but they do release the file handles to the system. An unclosed file may have buffered data that does not get written, or, in the case of a newly created file, it might not be added to the file system's directory of files.

fclose

A program closes a file by calling the *fclose* function. The argument is the FILE pointer that the *fopen* function returned, as shown here:

```
FILE *fp = fopen("data.txt", "r");  /* open a file */
/* ... */
fclose(fp);                         /* close the file */
```

Sequential Access

Text stream files are usually accessed sequentially. Programs read input text files beginning with the first character and continuing serially through the text until reaching end-of-file. Programs usually create new text files sequentially, too, writing characters from beginning to end. The functions that read and write the console have corresponding file functions.

getc, putc, fgetc, and *fputc*

These functions are similar to *getchar* and *putchar* except that they include FILE pointer arguments. The two forms are identical in that *getc* and *fgetc* do the same thing as do *putc* and *fputc*. Exercise 7.2 creates a text file and writes data into it. Then it closes, reopens, and reads the file and displays its contents to standard output.

EXERCISE 7.2 *fgetc and fputc.*

```c
#include <stdio.h>

int main()
{
    char msg[] = "This is a stream of test data";

    char *cp = msg;
    int c;
    /* --- create a text file --- */
    FILE *fp = fopen("test.dat", "w");
    if (fp != NULL) {
        /* --- write text to the file one char at a time --- */
        while (*cp)
            fputc(*cp++, fp);
        /* --- close the output file --- */
        fclose(fp);
    }
    /* --- open the file for input --- */
    fp = fopen("test.dat", "r");
    if (fp != NULL) {
        /* --- read text from the file one char at a time --- */
        while ((c = fgetc(fp)) != EOF)
            putchar(c);
        /* --- close the input file --- */
        fclose(fp);
    }
}
```

If you were to substitute the global device identifiers *stdin* in calls to *fgetc*, and *stdout* in calls to *fputc*, they would be the functional equivalents of *getchar* and *putchar*.

ungetc

C includes the *ungetc* function, which pushes a character into an input stream so that it is the next character read from that stream. Only one pushed character between reads of a file is guaranteed to work. Here is an example of a call to *ungetc*:

```c
ungetc('X', stdin);  /* push 'X' into standard input */
```

Programmers use *ungetc* in text-parsing algorithms when a parsing scan has proceeded one character past a lexical sequence. The program identifies the end of the lexical sequence by the presence of a character that does not contribute to the current sequence but is the start of the next one.

To demonstrate, we revisit the recursive descent calculator from Exercises 4.14 and 6.3. This time, instead of reading the expression into a memory array and parsing the array, we will parse one character at a time as it is typed in. When each operator function and the *number* function reach characters that terminate their scan, they call *ungetc* to return the terminal character to the stream so that it is available to the next scan in the descent.

EXERCISE 7.3 *Parsing with **ungetc**.*

```
#include <stdio.h>
#include <ctype.h>
#include <setjmp.h>

/* ---- prototypes ---- */
int addsubt(void);
int multdiv(void);
int number(void);
void error(void);

/* --- error jmp_buf buffer --- */
jmp_buf errjb;

int pos;

int main()
{
    int ans = -1, c;
    while (ans != 0)    {
        /* --- mark the top of the parsing descent --- */
        if (setjmp(errjb) == 0) {
            pos = 0;
            /* ---- read an expression ----- */
            puts("\nEnter expression (0 to quit): ");
            /* --- evaluate the expression --- */
            ans = addsubt();
            if (getchar() != '\n')
                error();
            printf("%d", ans);
        }
        else    {
```

continued

Exercise 7.3 *Parsing with **ungetc** (continued).*

```
                /* --- an error occurred --- */
                while (getchar() != '\n')
                    ;
                printf("\nTry again");
            }
        }
        return 0;
    }
    /* ---- top of recursive descent: add/subtract ---- */
    int addsubt()
    {
        int rtn = multdiv();
        int op;
        while ((op = getchar())== '+' || op == '-') {
            int opr2 = multdiv();
            if (op == '+')
                rtn += opr2;
            else
                rtn -= opr2;
            pos++;
        }
        ungetc(op, stdin);
        return rtn;
    }
    /* ---- highest precedence: multiply/divide ---- */
    int multdiv()
    {
        int rtn = number();
        int op;
        while ((op = getchar()) == '*' || op == '/')     {
            int opr2 = number();
            if (op == '*')
                rtn *= opr2;
            else
                rtn /= opr2;
            pos++;
        }
        ungetc(op, stdin);
        return rtn;
    }
```

continued

Exercise 7.3 *Parsing with **ungetc** (continued).*

```
/* ---- extract a number ---- */
int number()
{
    int rtn = 0;
    int c = getchar();
    if (c == '(')    {
        /* --- parenthetical expression --- */
        pos++;
        rtn = addsubt();              /* back to top   */
        if (getchar() != ')')         /* must have ')' */
            error();
        pos++;
        return rtn;
    }
    /* --- extract the number --- */
    if (!isdigit(c))
        error();
    while (isdigit(c))   {

        rtn = rtn * 10 + c - '0';
        c = getchar();
        pos++;
    }
    ungetc(c, stdin);
    return rtn;
}
/* ---- syntax error ---- */
void error(void)
{
    putchar('\r');
    while (pos--)          /* position error pointer */
        putchar(' ');
    printf("^ syntax error");
    longjmp(errjb, 1);  /* return to top of program */
}
```

fgets and fputs

The *fgets* function reads a string into memory. The first argument is the address of a buffer. The second argument is the length of the buffer, and the third is the FILE pointer. The *fgets* function reads characters up to one minus the value of the second argument. If it finds a newline character in the input stream, the function transfers the newline character into the buffer and stops reading. That behavior is different from that of *gets*, which does not copy the terminating newline into memory. The *fgets* function copies a null character into memory after the last character is read from the stream. Here is the *fgets* prototype:

```
char *fgets(void *buf, int len, FILE *fp);
```

The *fputs* function writes a null-terminated string to the output stream. Unlike *puts*, *fputs* does not append a newline character to the output stream. Here is the *fputs* prototype:

```
int fputs(const char *buf, FILE *fp);
```

Exercise 7.4 uses *fgets* to read the **test.dat** file created by Exercise 7.2 and writes the first 10 characters to standard output by using *fputs*.

EXERCISE 7.4 *The **fgets** and **fputs** functions.*

```
#include <stdio.h>

int main()
{
    char buf[10];
    FILE *fp = fopen("test.dat", "r");
    if (fp != NULL) {
        fgets(buf, 10, fp);
        fputs(buf, stdout);
        fclose(fp);
    }
    return 0;
}
```

The *fgets* function returns the address of its buffer argument unless there is an input error or the read starts at or past the end-of-file position, whereupon *fgets* returns a *NULL* pointer. Exercise 7.5 uses *fgets* and *fputs* to copy its own source code file to another file.

```
#include <stdio.h>

int main()
{
    char buf[80];
    FILE *fi = fopen("ex07005.c", "r");
    if (fi != NULL )      {
        FILE *fo = fopen("ex07005.sav", "w");
        if (fo != NULL) {
            while (fgets(buf, 80, fi) != NULL)
                fputs(buf, fo);
            fclose(fo);
        }
        fclose(fi);
    }
    return 0;
}
```

fflush

The *fflush* function flushes the output stream specified by its FILE pointer argument, as shown in this prototype:

```
int fflush(FILE *fp);
```

Random Access

A random-access file is one that you can access by first positioning the file pointer to a specific location in the file. Such files are usually recorded as binary files and consist of fixed-length records. To proceed through this lesson, first we will build a data file of employee records. Because several programs will share a structure definition and some functions, we build our first local header file to be included in the programs we write along with the standard library header files. That file, **employee.h**, follows:

```
#include <stdio.h>
#include <string.h>

/* --- employee record format --- */
struct employee {
    int emplno;
    char name[25];
    float salary;
};

typedef struct employee Employee;

#define FILENAME "employee.dat"

/* ---- get an employee number from the user ---- */
int GetEmployeeNo(void)
{
    int emplno;
    printf("Enter next empl# (0 to quit): ");
    scanf("%d", &emplno);
    return emplno;
}

int GetEmployeeData(Employee *emp)
{
    memset(emp->name, 0, sizeof emp->name);
    printf("\nEnter name (end to skip):   ");
    scanf("%s", &emp->name);
    if (strcmp(emp->name, "end"))    {
        printf("Enter salary: ");
        scanf("%f", &emp->salary);
        return 1;
    }
    return 0;
}

void DisplayEmployeeRecord(const Employee *emp)
{
    printf("\nEmpl#:  %d",    emp->emplno);
    printf("\nName:   %s",    emp->name);
    printf("\nSalary: %5.2f", emp->salary);
}

void SeekEmployeeRecord(FILE *fp, int emplno)
{
    long fpos = (emplno-1)*sizeof(Employee);
    fseek(fp, fpos, SEEK_SET);
}
```

This header file contains the *Employee* structure, a global symbol that defines the data file name, and several functions shared by the exercises that follow.

N O T E

The **employee.h** header file is unlike the header files that you will build with conventional C compilers in that it contains executable code. Quincy is an interpreter and has no link process. In the conventional environment, header files declare external variables, data structures, and function prototypes that are shared by independently compiled translation units, which are later linked to form a single executable program. Because Quincy has no linker, each program consists of only one translation unit, which itself consists of the principal source code file and all included header files. We use header files such as **employee.h** to emulate a linker environment.

fwrite

The *fwrite* function, which figures prominently in the next exercise, is declared this way:

```
int fwrite(const void *buf, int len, int num, FILE *fp);
```

The first argument is the address of the buffer, the second is the length of a logical record, the third is the number of logical records written by this call, and the last argument is the FILE pointer.

Exercise 7.6 collects data from the console and builds a file of fixed-length binary records by using the *fwrite* function.

EXERCISE 7.6 *The **fwrite** function.*

```
#include "employee.h"

int main()
{
    /* --- open output file --- */
    FILE *fp = fopen(FILENAME, "wb");
    Employee emp;
    int empno = 0;
    if (fp != NULL) {
        /* --- read employee record from console --- */
        while (GetEmployeeData(&emp))    {
            /* --- write the employee record --- */
            printf("Employee # is %d", ++empno);
            emp.emplno = empno;
            fwrite(&emp, sizeof emp, 1, fp);
        }
        fclose(fp);
    }
    return 0;
}
```

Observe the *#include* statement for **employee.h**. It encloses the filename in double quotes rather than using angle brackets as the others do. That convention tells the compiler that the header files are not a part of the compiler package and that it should look for the header in the application source code subdirectory.

Observe also that Exercise 7.6 does not include **stdio.h** even though it uses several functions declared in that header file. Because **employee.h** includes **stdio.h**, Exercise 7.6 does not have to.

Exercise 7.6 collects employee names and salaries and builds employee records. The program assigns employee numbers as a function of the physical location of the record in the file. These employee numbers will allow you to retrieve the employee records in a later exercise.

fread

The *fread* function reads records that *fwrite* writes. Here is the *fread* prototype:

```
int fread(const void *buf, int len, int num, FILE *fp);
```

The arguments have the same meaning as those in *fwrite*. The *fread* function returns the number of items read or zero on end-of-file.

Exercise 7.7 reads and displays the records in the file that Exercise 7.6 created.

EXERCISE 7.7 *The **fread** function.*

```
#include "employee.h"

int main()
{
    /* --- open input file --- */
    FILE *fp = fopen(FILENAME, "rb");
    Employee emp;
    if (fp != NULL) {
        while (fread(&emp, sizeof emp, 1, fp) != 0)
            DisplayEmployeeRecord(&emp);
        fclose(fp);
    }
    return 0;
}
```

fseek

So far, we have accessed our random-access employee file sequentially only. We can, however, access the records in random order as well by using the *fseek* function. The *fseek* function changes the file position for the next read or write operation by providing a new character offset into the file. The *fseek* function has this prototype:

```
int fseek(FILE *fp, long offset, int where);
```

The first argument is the FILE pointer. The second argument is a relative byte offset—which may be positive or negative—that will change the file position. The third argument specifies how the offset is to be applied. It is one of the global values in Table 7.3.

TABLE 7.3 *fseek offset operands.*

GLOBAL	SEEK TO OFFSET FROM:
SEEK_SET	beginning of file
SEEK_CUR	current file position
SEEK_END	end of file

Exercise 7.8 is a random-access program that retrieves employee records by employee number—which the user provides—and then allows the user to update the matching employee record. The program calls the *SeekEmployeeRecord* function, which is defined in employee.h. Refer to that listing to see how the *fseek* function repositions the file pointer.

EXERCISE 7.8 *Update mode and the fseek function.*

```
#include "employee.h"

int main()
{
    /* --- open input file --- */
    FILE *fp = fopen(FILENAME, "r+b");
    Employee emp = { 1 };
    if (fp != NULL) {
        while (emp.emplno != 0) {
```

continued

EXERCISE **7.8** *Update mode and the **fseek** function (continued).*

```
                /* --- read employee record from console --- */
                if ((emp.emplno = GetEmployeeNo()) != 0)    {
                    SeekEmployeeRecord(fp, emp.emplno);
                    if (fread(&emp, sizeof emp, 1, fp) != 0)     {
                        /* --- display employee record --- */
                        DisplayEmployeeRecord(&emp);
                        /* --- collect changes --- */
                        if (GetEmployeeData(&emp))   {
                            /* --- write the employee record --- */
                            SeekEmployeeRecord(fp, emp.emplno);
                            fwrite(&emp, sizeof emp, 1, fp);
                        }
                    }
                }
            }
        fclose(fp);
    }
    return 0;
}
```

There are many other things that an employee file maintenance program would do, such as add new employees and delete employee records of those who leave employment. Consider how you would modify Exercise 7.8 and perhaps the employee file structure to make those changes.

ftell

The exercises so far have implied that random access, binary data mode, and fixed-length records go hand in hand and that sequential access, text data mode, and variable-length records are inseparable. Neither implication is true. You can have any mix of access method, text mode, and record length.

This leads us to the *ftell* function, which reports the current file position as an offset that a program can use later to reposition the file to a previous location. Here is the *ftell* prototype:

```
long ftell(FILE *fp);
```

Sometimes the position of a file record cannot be computed from a fixed record length. This is particularly true of text files that consist of lines of text such as those processed by a text editor program. To illustrate, Exercise 7.9 reads a text file, which you name on the command line, and stores the file position, as reported by the *ftell* function of each of the lines of text in an array. Then it uses the array to locate a chosen line number and display its value on standard output.

```
#include <stdio.h>

#define MAXLINES 200
#define MAXBUFLEN 100

long LineOffset[MAXLINES];
int linectr;
char buf[MAXBUFLEN];

void LoadOffsets(FILE *fp);
int GetLineNo(void);
void DisplayLine(FILE *fp, int lno);

int main(int argc, char *argv[])
{
    if (argc > 1)    {
        FILE *fp;
        int lno;
        if ((fp = fopen(argv[1], "r")) != NULL)       {
            LoadOffsets(fp);
            while ((lno = GetLineNo()) != 0)
                DisplayLine(fp, lno);
            fclose(fp);
        }
    }
    return 0;
}
/* --- build a table of offsets to text lines --- */
void LoadOffsets(FILE *fp)
{
    while (linectr < MAXLINES)  {
        LineOffset[linectr++] = ftell(fp);
        if (fgets(buf, MAXBUFLEN, fp) == NULL)
            break;
    }
}
/* --- get the line number to display --- */
int GetLineNo(void)
{
    int lno;
    printf("\nEnter line # (0 to quit): ");
    scanf("%d", &lno);
    if (lno < 0 || lno >= MAXLINES)
        lno = 0;
    return lno;
}
/* --- display the line number --- */
void DisplayLine(FILE *fp, int lno)
{
    fseek(fp, LineOffset[lno-1], SEEK_SET);
    if (fgets(buf, MAXBUFLEN, fp) != NULL)
        puts(buf);
}
```

Don't forget to put the input file name on the command line before running the program. You can use one of the exercise source code files. For example, **ex07009.c** is the name of the source code file for Exercise 7.9.

N O T E   Observe the *#define* definitions in Exercise 7.9. They equate identifiers and values. In this case, they define the maximum number of lines of text that the program will read from the file and the maximum line length expected. We use *#define* this way to isolate global values, particularly those that are used many times, and to give them mnemonic names so that their usage will help to explain their meaning. If you decide to change those values, you have only to change the definitions. The rest of the program will adjust when you recompile it.

rewind

The *rewind* function, shown in the following prototype, is one of convenience. It positions the file pointer to the beginning of the file and is the same as coding *fseek(fp, 0L, SEEK_SET)*:

```
void rewind(FILE *fp);
```

Formatted Input/Output

You can read formatted data from files and send formatted data to files just as you do with standard input and output. File input/output has functions that correspond to *scanf* and *printf*.

fscanf and fprintf

Here are the prototypes for the standard *fscanf* and *fprintf* functions:

```
int fscanf(FILE *fp, const char *fmt, ...);
int fprintf(FILE *fp, const char *fmt, ...);
```

These functions work exactly like *scanf* and *printf* except that they read and write the files specified as their first argument rather than *stdin* and *stdout*.

The *scanf* function depends on what the user types, which could be significantly different from what the formatting string is expecting. You have more control over what is in the text data file that *fscanf* reads.

Printing

Printing is a matter of writing to the printer device just as you do to other files. The ANSI standard does not specify exactly how a program prints, leaving that detail to the operating system and the C language implementation. Programs running under MS-DOS have several ways that they can print. They can open files named "prn", "lpt1", "lpt2", and so on, and they can direct output to *stdprn*, the standard print device. Quincy supports all these printing techniques.

Formatting a report is a matter of using *fprintf* in meaningful ways. Exercise 7.10 reads the **employee.dat** file and prints its contents.

EXERCISE 7.10 *fprintf and printing.*

```
#include "employee.h"

#define PAGELEN 50

void PrintHeader(void);
void PrintEmployeeRecord(Employee *emp);

int main()
{
    /* --- open input file --- */
    FILE *fp = fopen(FILENAME, "rb");
    Employee emp;
    if (fp != NULL) {
        PrintHeader();
        while (fread(&emp, sizeof emp, 1, fp) != 0)
            PrintEmployeeRecord(&emp);
        fputc('\f', stdprn);
        fclose(fp);
    }
    return 0;
}
```

continued

EXERCISE 7.10 *fprintf* and printing (continued).

```
void PrintHeader()
{
    static int pageno = 0;
    fprintf(stdprn, "\rEmpl#  Name           Salary  Page %d",
            ++pageno);
    fprintf(stdprn, "\r\n-----  -------------  ------- ");
}

void PrintEmployeeRecord(Employee *emp)
{
    static int linectr = 0;
    if (linectr++ == PAGELEN)   {
        /* --- bottom of page --- */
        fputc('\f', stdprn);
        PrintHeader();
        linectr = 0;
    }
    fprintf(stdprn, "\r\n%5d  %-13.13s %5.2f",
        emp->emplno, emp->name, emp->salary);
}
```

Observe that the print strings include the "\r" escape sequence in front of each newline character. Output to *stdprn* does not do text translation because printers use the "\n" character as a normal line feed. You have to include the extra "\r" carriage return character to return the print position to the left margin.

The "\f" escape sequence character is a form feed to advance the printer to the next page.

Managing Files

The standard input/output library includes functions that allow your program to manage its files. Included are functions to rename files, remove files, and create temporary files.

rename

The *rename* function, shown in the following prototype, changes the name of a file that is not currently open:

```
int rename(const char *oldfile, const char newfile*);
```

remove

The *remove* function, shown in the following prototype, deletes a named file:

```
int remove(const char *filename);
```

Exercise 7.11 deletes the three working files that exercises in this chapter built.

EXERCISE 7.11 *The remove function.*

```
#include <stdio.h>

int main()
{
    remove("test.dat");
    remove("ex07005.sav");
    remove("employee.dat");
    return 0;
}
```

tmpfile

The *tmpfile* function, shown in the following prototype, creates and opens a temporary file:

```
FILE *tmpfile(void);
```

The temporary file is opened with update access in binary mode ("w+b"). When you close the file or when the program terminates, the system deletes the temporary file.

tmpnam

The *tmpnam* function, shown in the following prototype, creates a unique temporary file name:

```
char *tmpnam(char *filename);
```

You can use the name to create a temporary file that you can later delete or rename. Programs that do extensive updates of files with the potential of an exceptional interruption (such as a power failure) often build the new data into a temporary file. When the update is complete and the file's integrity is ensured, the program deletes the prior version of the file and renames the temporary file.

Summary

In this chapter you learned about standard input/output devices and how to redirect them to disk files. Then you learned how to create disk files, write data into them, retrieve the data, change it, print it, rename the files, and delete the files.

Chapter 8

THE C PREPROCESSOR

The term *preprocessor* designates a process that reads source code, performs some preliminary translation of that code, and writes new source code to be read by the compiler. It is a preprocessor because it processes source code before the compiler does.

The C language has no built-in facilities for including other source files during the compile, for defining macros, or for compile-time directives that include some lines of code and exclude others based on conditions. Those capabilities are provided by the C preprocessor, which, although it is integrated with most contemporary compilers, is regarded as a process independent of the compiler. The preprocessor reads source code, looks for preprocessing directive statements and macro invocations, and translates the source code accordingly. It also eliminates program comments and excess white space.

Quincy implements the preprocessor as an integral part of the interpreter program. This chapter describes how to use preprocessing directives in a program. You will learn about:

▼ Including files

▼ Writing macros

▼ Compile-time conditional directives

Preprocessing Directives

Preprocessing directives are lines of code that begin with a pound sign (#). The pound sign must be the first character on a line of code after any optional white space. The directive keyword follows, with optional white space between it and the pound sign. The entire line is devoted to the directive, which affects the translation of the source code to be passed to the compiler. Table 8.1 lists the preprocessing directives that Quincy supports and that I teach in this chapter.

TABLE 8.1 *Preprocessing directives.*

DIRECTIVE	MEANING
#	Null directive, no action
#include	Include a source code file
#define	Define a macro
#undef	Remove the definition of a macro
#if	Compile code if condition is true
#ifdef	Compile code if macro is defined
#ifndef	Compile code if macro is not defined
#else	Compile code if previous #if... condition is not true
#elif	Compile code if previous #if... condition is not true and current condition is true
#endif	Terminate #if...#else conditional block
#error	Stop compiling and display error message

Preprocessing directives are effective beginning with their position in the translation unit and continuing until another directive changes their meaning.

Including Files

A translation unit is an independently compiled program module consisting of the C source code file and any other source code files that the program includes.

By convention, C source code files, have a **.c** file name extension and include header source code files, which have a **.h** file name extension. All the functions are in the C source code file. Header files contain declarations that are shared among translation units. Header files typically declare external variables, structure and union formats, macros, and function prototypes. Header files do not contain any function or variable definitions. In other words, header files, which can be included in multiple translation units that are linked into a single program, do not define anything that reserves memory.

NOTE Programs developed with Quincy do not always follow that convention because Quincy does not produce programs from multiple translation units. Therefore, functions that are used by many programs are placed in their associated header files. Most of the standard library functions are not, because they are implemented from within the Quincy interpreter. Common functions that support the exercise applications, such as the menu and data entry screen drivers in Chapter 9, are coded in the header files that declare them.

#include

The *#include* preprocessing directive includes the named file in the translation unit, replacing the directive. You can have multiple levels of includes. That is, an included file can include other files. Standard C requires that a conforming compiler supports nesting of up to eight levels of included header files. Quincy supports ten levels.

The preprocessor does not detect and suppress inclusion of a file that has already been included in a translation unit. This is done on purpose to allow compile-time conditionals to modify subsequent inclusions of header files:

```
#define MODHEADER
#include "table.c"
#undef MODHEADER
#include "table.c"
```

To avoid the problems associated with multiple inclusions of a header file that should be included only once, you can use these compile-time conditional controls in a header file:

```
/* --- myhdr.h --- */
#ifndef MYHDR_H
#define MYHDR_H

/* the header file information ... */

#endif
```

There are two ways to include header files in a program:

```
#include <stdio.h>
#include "menus.h"
```

The first usage surrounds the file name with "less-than" and "greater-than" symbols. This notation tells the compiler to search for the header file among the header files that came with the compiler. The second usage surrounds the file name with double quotes. This notation tells the compiler to search for the header file among the source code of the application being compiled; if it does not find it, it is to search the compiler's header files.

The underlying theory is that a compiler, which is installed in a public subdirectory, compiles applications that are installed in their own private subdirectories. The applications include the compiler's public header files and their own private header files. The two notations allow the compiler to discern the one common set of header files from the many other sets.

Macros

A macro defines a meaning for an identifier. The most common usage defines a global symbol that represents a value. A second usage defines macros with parameters that, when invoked, resemble function calls but that generate in-line substitution of the invoking statement's arguments with the macro definition's parameters.

#define

The *#define* preprocessing directive defines a macro. In its simpler format, the directive declares an identifier and adds code that replaces the identifier wherever it appears in subsequent source code. Such macros isolate global value definitions, assigning mnemonic identifiers, as this example illustrates:

```
#define MAXNBRS 10
int narray[MAXNBRS];
for (i = 0; i < MAXNBRS; i++)
    /* ... */
```

In this example, the MAXNBRS symbol has meaning to the programmer who reads the code. It is a mnemonic value associated with the maximum number of entries in that particular array. You might use the value many places in the program. By convention, some programmers use all uppercase letters to identify these macros. It tells them that they are looking at a macro invocation rather than a variable identifier when they see the identifier used in code.

If you decide later that the array needs to be a different size, you can change the macro and recompile the program. If the macro is used in more than one translation unit, you code the macro into a header file and include the header in all the source code files that use the macro. Then, to change the value, you change the macro in the header file, recompile all the translation units, and relink the executable program. The idea is to isolate potential global changes into one source code location and to assign meaningful mnemonic symbols to what might otherwise be meaningless numerical values.

The substituted value can be a constant expression, and it can include identifiers that are declared in previous macros, as shown in this example:

```
#define SCREENHEIGHT 25
#define SCREENWIDTH 80
#define SCREENBUFFER (SCREENHEIGHT*SCREENWIDTH)
```

Observe the parentheses around the macro definition's expression. These are not necessary, but they are prudent. Consider this example:

```
#define HEIGHT bottom-top+1
area=width*HEIGHT;
```

The preprocessor would emit this code for the statement:

```
area=width*bottom-top+1;
```

Due to the rules of precedence, the result would probably be wrong. Here is how you should define the macro and how it would be expanded:

```
#define HEIGHT (bottom-top+1)
area=width*HEIGHT;              /* as coded    */

area=width*(bottom-top+1;)  /* as expanded */
```

You can define a macro that expands to a string constant, as shown here:

```
#define VERSION "Version 4.1\nCopyright (c) 1994"
puts(VERSION);
```

#define with Arguments

Macros with parameters resemble functions that are expanded in-line, but they do not work exactly like function calls. Consider this example:

```
#define Cube(x) ((x)*(x)*(x))
```

The *x* parameter can be replaced by any numerical expression including one with a function call. Observe again the parentheses. The complete expansion is enclosed in parentheses to preserve the integrity of its argument in the context of an enclosing expression. So are the macro parameters, for the same reason. Here is a typical, safe use of the *Cube* macro:

```
height = 123;
volume = Cube(height);
```

Here are some unsafe uses of *Cube*:

```
volume = Cube(height++);
randomvolume = Cube(rand());
```

If *Cube* were a function, these statements would be correct. However, because *Cube* is a macro, these usages have side effects. Their arguments are more than simple expressions; they do other things. The first usage auto-increments the argument and would be expanded this way:

```
volume = ((height++)*(height++)*(height++));
```

If height starts off with a value of 123, the effective expression would be this:

```
volume = 123*124*125;
```

The second unsafe usage involves a function call. The preprocessor would expand it to this code:

```
randomvolume = ((rand())*(rand())*(rand()))
```

At best, this code is less efficient than it needs to be because it calls the *rand* function three times. This example is a worst case, however, because the code produces the wrong result. The *rand* function returns a different value for each call, and the result is not the volume of anything meaningful.

How would you use the *Cube* macro safely to produce the correct results? You must remove the side effects by moving their actions outside the macro calls:

```
volume = Cube(height);
height++;
randomheight = rand();
randomvolume = Cube(randomheight);
```

A macro's parameters can include expressions and references to previously defined macros, making for some exotic macro definitions. Consider Exercise 8.1, which follows.

EXERCISE 8.1 *Macros.*

```
#include <stdio.h>

#define OVERTIME      1.5
#define TAXRATE       0.15
#define WKWEEK        40
#define REG(h)        ((h) < WKWEEK ? (h) : WKWEEK)
#define OTIME(h)      ((h) < WKWEEK ? 0 : h - WKWEEK)
#define OTIMEPAY(h,r) ((r) * OTIME(h) * OVERTIME)
#define REGPAY(h,r)   ((r) * REG(h))
#define GROSSPAY(h,r) (OTIMEPAY(h,r) + REGPAY(h,r))
#define WHOLDING(h,r) (GROSSPAY(h,r) * TAXRATE)
#define NETPAY(h,r)   (GROSSPAY(h,r) - WHOLDING(h,r))
```

continued

Exercise 8.1 *Macros (continued).*

```
int main()
{
    int hours;
    float rate;
    printf("Enter hours (xx) rate (x.xx): ");
    scanf("%d %f", &hours, &rate);
    printf("\nRegular:    %5.2f", REGPAY(hours, rate));
    printf("\nOvertime:   %5.2f", OTIMEPAY(hours, rate));
    printf("\nGross:      %5.2f", GROSSPAY(hours, rate));
    printf("\nWitholding: %5.2f", WHOLDING(hours, rate));
    printf("\nNet Pay:    %5.2f", NETPAY(hours, rate));
    return 0;
}
```

The macros in Exercise 8.1 cooperate to compute values for a payroll. Read the macros carefully as you follow this explanation. The first three macros define constant global values, assigning identifiers to the values for the overtime rate (*OVERTIME*), tax withholding rate (*TAXRATE*), and the number of regular hours in a work week (*WKWEEK*).

The *REG* macro computes the number of regular (non-overtime) hours from the total number of hours worked that week. The expression returns the actual hours if they are less than a work week. Otherwise, it returns the number of hours in a work week.

The *OTIME* macro computes the number of overtime hours from the total hours worked. If the hours worked are less than a work week, the value returned is zero; otherwise, it is the difference between the hours worked and a work week.

The *OTIMEPAY* macro computes the amount of overtime pay from the hours worked and the hourly wage. It multiplies the wage times the overtime hours times the overtime rate.

The *REGPAY* macro computes the amount of regular pay from the hours worked and the hourly wage. It multiplies the wage times the regular hours.

Observe that these macros call previously defined macros.

The *GROSSPAY* macro computes the sum of the overtime and regular pay from the hours worked and the hourly wage.

The *WHOLDING* macro computes the amount of taxes to withhold from the hours worked and the hourly wage. It multiplies the gross pay times the tax withholding rate.

The *NETPAY* macro computes the net pay from the hours worked and the hourly wage. It computes the difference between gross pay and withholding.

The program reads the number of hours worked and the hourly wage from standard input and displays the results on standard output. Following is a typical session:

```
Enter hours (xx) rate (x.xx): 45 18.50

Regular:    740.00
Overtime:   138.75
Gross:      878.75
Witholding: 131.81
Net Pay:    746.94
```

You can modify the algorithm by changing any of the first three constants and recompiling the program. In a real payroll program, tax rates are based on the employee's salary, number of dependents, and whatever tables the IRS has in effect for the current year.

All the macros with parameters could have been functions. What is the advantage of using macros? First, a macro expands to inline code. There is no function call overhead involved when you call a macro. Macros that are used often should, therefore, not expand to a lot of code because every call to them is an individual expansion.

You can make a macro look more like a function by using the backslash character (\) as a line continuation operator in the macro definition, as shown in Exercise 8.2.

EXERCISE 8.2 *Macro line continuation.*

```c
#include <stdio.h>
#include <time.h>

#define DisplayTitle(a)                                \
{                                                      \
    time_t now = time(NULL);                           \
    printf(a);                                         \
    printf(" as of %s", asctime(localtime(&now)));     \
}

int main()
{
    DisplayTitle("Hourly Report");
    return 0;
}
```

Observe that all the lines in the macro definition except the last line are terminated with a backslash. Recall that a preprocessing directive occupies only one line of code. The backslash character acts as a line continuation operator within a macro definition so that a particularly long macro definition does not extend well out of sight past the right margin of your programmer's editor.

The braces in the *DisplayTitle* macro are redundant, but only when viewed in the way that it is called in the exercise. The macro call is the first statement in a statement block, so its *time_t* declaration does not need a defined block. If you precede the call with other non-declarator statements, the braces in the macro are necessary.

Even when a macro does not have a declarator, if it does have more than one statement, you should surround them with braces. This convention allows you to code the macro call as the only statement controlled by a conditional test, as shown here:

```
if (whatever)
    DisplayTitle("Hello");
```

Without the braces in the macro definition, only its first statement would execute as a result of the condition. The others would execute regardless of the value of the condition.

THE # "STRINGIZING" OPERATOR

The # operator within a macro definition converts into a string the argument for the parameter that follows. Consider an *Error* macro that displays the error code on standard output. Without the # operator, you could write the macro as shown here:

```
#define Error(n) printf("Error %d", n);
```

You can get the same effect by using the # operator, sometimes called the *stringizing* operator. Exercise 8.3 demonstrates that usage.

EXERCISE 8.3 *The # stringizing operator.*

```
#include <stdio.h>
#define Error(n) puts("Error " #n)
int main()
{
    Error(53);
    return 0;
}
```

The #n sequence in the macro definition tells the preprocessor to convert into a string whatever is passed as an argument. The macro call has 53 as the argument, so the macro is expanded this way:

```
puts("Error " "53");
```

The adjacent strings are concatenated (pasted together) according to the syntax for string constants, and the effective statement is this:

```
puts("Error 53");
```

If you wonder about how the # operator could be used, consider the *assert* macro as it is defined in **assert.h**:

```
#define assert(n) (n)?((void)0):(_assertfail(#n))
```

The *assert* macro tests the condition that you provide as an argument. If the condition is true, the macro does nothing. If it is false, the macro calls the system-defined *_assertfail* function and passes a string that it builds with the # operator. The string is the text of the condition that failed the assertion, which is how Exercise 6.1 was able to produce this message on the console:

```
assert failed: (msg != NULL) File: ex06001.c, Line: 25
```

THE ## OPERATOR

The ## operator concatenates arguments. The preprocessor takes the arguments that match the parameter references on either side of the ## operator and turns them into a single token. Exercise 8.4 is an example.

EXERCISE **8.4** *The ## token pasting operator.*

```
#include <stdio.h>

#define BkChapVerse(b,c,v) b ## c ## v
int main()
{
    unsigned bcv = BkChapVerse(5,12,43);
    printf("%u", bcv);
    return 0;
}
```

The program displays the value 51243, which is the constant long integer that results when you paste the three arguments 5, 12, and 43.

Understand that you don't get the same results by passing variables with those values to the macro. The macro is expanded by the preprocessor, which would paste the names of the variables rather than some future values that they might contain.

After the concatenation, the resulting value is scanned again by the pre-processor, so you can use the facility to build some complex—if not bizarre—macros. Exercise 8.5 is a demonstration.

EXERCISE **8.5** *More ## pasting.*

```
#include <stdio.h>

#define AbleBaker "alpha bravo"
#define cat(a,b)   a ## b

int main()
{
    puts(cat(Able, Baker));
    return 0;
}
```

The *AbleBaker* macro defines a string value. The *cat* macro is a general-purpose two-argument concatenation macro. The *puts* function call invokes the *cat* macro with the arguments *Able* and *Baker*. Those arguments concatenate to form the single identifier *AbleBaker*, which is then expanded into the string constant "alpha bravo", which gets passed to the *puts* function.

Do not be concerned if you are confused by all this. Few programmers understand ## until they need it or see it used meaningfully in a way that is relevant to a problem at hand. Most programmers never need it.

#undef

The *#undef* preprocessor directive removes the definition of a macro for the ensuing source code lines in the translation unit. You use this when you want the meaning of the identifier to return to its default meaning or when you want to change the meaning. You cannot have multiple definitions of a macro in effect at the same time.

Compile-Time Conditional Directives

Compile-time conditional directives control which lines of code get compiled and which ones do not. You can control code compilation based on the value of an expression or on whether a particular macro has been defined.

#if

The *#if* directive tests the constant expression that follows the directive keyword. If the expression evaluates to true, the ensuing source code group, up to the next *#else*, *#elif*, or *#endif* is passed to the compiler. Otherwise, it is not.

#endif

This directive is the terminator for all *#if...* preprocessing directives. Exercise 8.6 demonstrates *#if* and *#endif*.

EXERCISE 8.6 *The **#if** and **#endif** preprocessing directives.*

```
#include <stdio.h>

#define DEBUG 1

int main()
{
#if DEBUG
    printf("\nDebugging");
#endif
    printf("\nRunning");
    return 0;
}
```

The line of code between the *#if* and the *#endif* compiles only if the expression *DEBUG* evaluates to a true value. In this case it does, because *DEBUG* is defined as a global integer constant with a value of 1. Use the Quincy editor to change the definition to this:

```
#define DEBUG 0
```

Now when you run the program, the line of code under control of the *#if*, *#endif* pair does not compile. The same thing happens if you remove the *#define* statement altogether.

You can test to see whether a macro is defined rather than testing its value, as shown in Exercise 8.7.

EXERCISE 8.7 *#if defined preprocessing directive.*

```
#include <stdio.h>

#define DEBUG

int main()
{
#if defined DEBUG
    printf("\nDebugging");
#endif
    printf("\nRunning");
    return 0;
}
```

To test that a macro is not defined, use this notation:

```
#if !defined DEBUG
```

#ifdef and #ifndef

The *#ifdef* and *#ifndef* directives are variations on *#if defined* and *#if !defined*, respectively. They work the same.

#else

You can code the *#else* directive after the statement group that is controlled by one of the *#if...* directives. The statement group that follows the *#else* compiles if the condition tested by the *#if...* is not true. One *#endif* directive terminates the two groups, as shown in Exercise 8.8.

EXERCISE 8.8 *The #else preprocessing directive.*

```
#include <stdio.h>

#define DEBUG

int main()
{
#if defined DEBUG
    printf("\nDebugging");
#else
    printf("\nNot debugging");
#endif
    printf("\nRunning");
    return 0;
}
```

#elif

The *#elif* preprocessing directive combines the effects of the *#else* and *#if* directives, as shown in Exercise 8.9.

EXERCISE 8.9 *The #elif preprocessing directive.*

```
#include <stdio.h>

#define DEBUG

int main()
{
#if defined DEBUG
    printf("\nDebugging");
#elif defined TESTING
    printf("\nTesting");
#elif defined EXPERIMENTAL
    printf("\nExperimental");
#else
    printf("\nNone of the above");
#endif
    printf("\nRunning");
    return 0;
}
```

#error

This directive causes the compiler to display an error message that includes whatever information you provide on the line past the directive keyword. It stops the compilation. It is typically used within the control of a compile-time conditional statement to alert the programmer that something is wrong in the way the compile has been set up. You can construct complex compile-time conditions with nested and mutually exclusive tests. The *#error* directive allows you to assert a compile-time error if the conditions are not logically organized. Exercise 8.10 is an example of this.

EXERCISE 8.10 *The #error preprocessing directive.*

```
#include <stdio.h>

#define DEBUG    1
#define TESTING 1

#if DEBUG & TESTING
   #error DEBUG & TESTING both have values
#endif

int main()
{
#if DEBUG
    printf("\nDebugging");
#elif TESTING
    printf("\nTesting");
#else
    printf("\nNot debugging");
#endif
    printf("\nRunning");
    return 0;
}
```

An alternative notation can be used when you are testing for the definition of macros rather than their values, as shown here:

```
#define DEBUG
#define TESTING

#ifdef DEBUG
  #ifdef TESTING
    #error DEBUG & TESTING both defined
  #endif
#endif
```

Other Standard Directives

Standard C defines two other preprocessing directives. Quincy does not support them.

#line

This directive lets you change the file name and line number that the compiler uses to report subsequent warning and error messages.

#pragma

This directive has no formal definition. Compilers may use it in ways that the compiler vendor sees fit. Typical uses are to suppress and enable certain annoying warning messages. For example, a compiler might issue warning messages if you do not reference a function argument in the function body. You might have a large number of functions called through a common function pointer, and not all of them use all the arguments. All of them must, however, declare the arguments so that their prototypes match the pointer declaration. You could use the compiler's custom *#pragma* to suppress the warning messages for those functions only.

Summary

In this chapter, you learned to include system and application header files, define macros, and use compile-time conditional directives.

Chapter 9

EXAMPLE PROGRAMS

*T*his chapter applies most of the lessons that you have learned about C programming to four example programs. Unlike the exercises in previous chapters—which were aimed at demonstrating C—these programs do real work. Each of them is a small application that you can use as is or modify and enhance to suit your own requirements.

Most applications operate within a framework that defines the user interface. Users must be able to select from the various processes that an application provides and enter data values for the application to use. The first of these requirements implies a *menu* process of one sort or another. The second implies the use of *data entry screens*. It is important to a sound system design that the format of menus and data entry screens be consistent throughout an application.

This chapter includes examples of menu and data entry screen functions. You can use them for small programs, particularly ones that are for your own use. However, programs that you develop for other users will probably run in established operating environments, such as Windows, and you will write your C programs within the framework of those systems.

This chapter also has an example program that searches the file directories for files that match a wild card specification. To cap things off, there is a tic-tac-toe game that you can play against the computer.

Console Input/Output

The standard input device is not always a good choice for interactive input/output such as menus and data entry screens. First, the program might use *stdin* and *stdout* for redirected input/output of disk files. Second, the buffered nature of standard input makes it particularly difficult for a program to control what the user enters and where the cursor is on the screen. Third, standard output has no provisions for clearing the screen and positioning the cursor. Fourth, standard input has no provisions for reading function keys from the keyboard.

N O T E

You can clear the screen and position the cursor with standard output on an MS-DOS computer if the ANSI.SYS device driver is loaded from the CONFIG.SYS start-up file. This technique is not reliable for programs that you distribute. You cannot be sure that every installation has ANSI.SYS loaded or even available, and some users would not understand how to install it.

In most cases, you need a nonportable mechanism for interactive input/output. Even relying on ANSI.SYS is nonportable. Many C compilers include a header file and library functions to support console input/output. That file is usually called **conio.h**, and Quincy implements the functions described here. Be aware that no standard definition exists for these functions or the operations that they support. The Quincy implementation reflects the way that I like to code for the console and includes the minimum suite of console functions needed to control a video display in text mode.

This approach is portable only to a degree. To move programs that use these five simple functions to a different type of computer or operating system you must rewrite them. Because they are small, simple, and isolated in a platform-dependent library, programs that depend on them can be ported to other platforms with a minimum of effort.

clrscr

The *clrscr* function, shown in the following prototype, clears the screen. The cursor is positioned in the upper left corner of the screen when the function returns.

```
void clrscr(void);
```

cprintf

The *cprintf* function, shown in the following prototype, is the console equivalent of standard output's *printf* function:

```
int cprintf(const char *, ...);
```

The *cprintf* function works just like *printf*, with this exception: with *cprintf*, the newline character ("\n") acts like a line feed instead of a carriage return, line feed character pair. It advances the cursor down one line without returning to the left margin. To get that behavior, you must send both characters ("\r\n") in the *cprintf* string.

Following the *cprintf* call, the screen cursor is positioned just past the last character displayed unless the last character was a carriage return or line feed.

cursor

The *cursor* function, shown in the following prototype, moves the screen cursor to the character position represented by its x,y coordinate arguments:

```
void cursor(int x, int y);
```

The coordinates are relative to zero. Position 0,0 is the upper left corner of the screen, and, on a 25 x 80 screen, position 79,24 is the bottom right corner.

The next call to *cprintf*, *getch*, or *putch* uses the new cursor position.

getch and *putch*

These functions, shown in the prototypes that follow, read characters from the keyboard and write characters to the screen at the current cursor position:

```
int getch(void);
void putch(int);
```

The *getch* function does not echo the character on the screen, does not advance the cursor, and returns as soon as the user presses a key. If the user presses a function key (**F1** through **F10**, **Home**, **Up**, **PgUp**, and so on), the key value returned has the most significant bit turned on. The **conio.h** header file defines global symbols for the values returned by the most common function keys.

The *getch* function works for many different key combinations, such as **Alt**, **Ctrl**, and **Shift** key combinations. If you want to use these keys in a program, you can determine the values that *getch* returns with a simple program such as this one:

```
#include <conio.h>

int main()
{
    int c = 0;
    while ((c = getch()) != ESC)
        cprintf("\r\n%d", c);
    return 0;
}
```

Type this program into Quincy (it is not among the exercises on the companion diskette), run it, and press the keys that you want to use. Write down the decimal values that the program displays for each one. Then add macros—such as the ones shown here—to your program or to **conio.h** to define global identifiers for the keys:

```
#define ALT_F1   232
#define CTRL_A     1
#define CTRL_END 245
```

The *putch* function displays its argument character on the screen at the current cursor character position and advances the cursor to the next character position.

Menus

A menu is a selection of commands from which the user chooses. You are accustomed to menu bars and pull-down menus with programs such as Quincy. Simpler programs—developed to run independently of any particular operating environment—display simple text menus on the screen and read the selections from the keyboard.

You can write custom code for menus each time that you use them, or you can use a general-purpose, reusable menu manager. The **menus.h** source code file, shown next, declares the function and data structure for a menu manager library function:

```
#ifndef MENUS_H
#define MENUS_H

#include <conio.h>

#define MLEFT 20
#define MTOP 5

/* ---- Menu Entry structure ---- */
typedef struct MenuEntry {
    char *name;
    void (*fn)(void);
} Menu;

void menuproc(char *ttl, Menu *mp);

#endif
```

The **menus.h** header file includes **conio.h**, which means that programs that include **menus.h** do not themselves have to include **conio.h**, although they may. The **menus.h** header file defines two macros that specify the left and top screen character coordinates where menus are displayed. It also declares a structure with a *typedef* of Menu. This structure defines the format of a single menu selection. It has pointers to the selection's text name and the function to be executed when the user chooses the menu selection. The header file also provides a prototype for the *menuproc* function shown next:

```
#include "menus.h"

/* ----- menu processor ----- */
void menuproc(char *ttl, Menu *mp)
{
    int i, sel = 0;
    while (sel != ESC)  {
        /* ---- clear the screen ---- */
        clrscr();
        /* ---- display the menu title ---- */
        cursor(MLEFT, MTOP);
        cprintf(ttl);
        /* ---- display menu selections ---- */
        for (i = 0; (mp+i)->name != NULL; i++)  {
            cursor(MLEFT, MTOP+i+2);
            cprintf("%3d: %s", i+1, (mp+i)->name);
        }
        cursor(MLEFT, MTOP+i+2);
        cprintf("Esc: Exit");
        /* ---- display selection prompt ---- */
        cursor(MLEFT, MTOP+i+4);
        cprintf("Select: ");
        /* --- get user's selection --- */
        if ((sel = getch()) != ESC) {
            putch(sel);
            sel -= '0';
            if (sel > 0 && sel < i+1)   {
                /* --- execute the selected function --- */
                ((mp+sel-1)->fn)();
                cursor(0,24);
                cprintf("Any key to continue...");
                getch();
            }
        }
    }
}
```

To add a menu to an application, you build an array of *Menu* structures that are initialized with text and function pointers. You pass the menu title and the address of the array to the *menuproc* function, which takes command of the program. It displays the menu, retrieves the user's selections, and calls the functions that match the selections, continuing to do so until the user presses the **Esc** key to terminate menu processing. Then the *menuproc* function returns.

N O T E In a traditional C programming environment, the *menuproc* function would be independently compiled and linked with your programs. Quincy has no linker, so the function is added to the **menus.h** header file that declares it.

Exercise 9.1 is a program that converts between Fahrenheit and Celsius temperatures. It uses a menu to let the user select which conversion to perform.

EXERCISE 9.1 *Using a menu.*

```c
#include <stdio.h>
#include "menus.h"

void FahrCels(void);
void CelsFahr(void);

int main()
{
    Menu menu[] = {
        {"Fahrenheit to Celsius", FahrCels},
        {"Celsius to Fahrenheit", CelsFahr},
        {NULL}
    };
    menuproc("Conversion Menu", menu);
    return 0;
}
void FahrCels(void)
{
    int Fahr;
    /* --- read Fahrenheit temperature from keyboard --- */
    printf("\nEnter temperature as Fahrenheit: ");
    scanf("%d", &Fahr);
    /* ---- display the result ---- */
    printf("%d Celsius",(5 * (Fahr - 32) / 9));
}
void CelsFahr(void)
{
    int Cels;
    /* --- read Fahrenheit temperature from keyboard --- */
    printf("\nEnter temperature as Celsius: ");
    scanf("%d", &Cels);
    /* ---- display the result ---- */
    printf("%d Fahrenheit", Cels * 9 / 5 + 32);
}
```

The *Menu* array in the *main* function of Exercise 9.1 defines two menu selections. Their functions are prototyped at the beginning of the program and defined just past the *main* function. When you first run the program, it displays this menu on the screen:

```
Conversion Menu

    1: Fahrenheit to Celsius
    2: Celsius to Fahrenheit
Esc: Exit

Select:
```

The *menuproc* function builds the menu and displays it by using the title and the entries in the *Menu* array. It adds the **Exit** selection and the **Select** prompt. By pressing **1** you see this message (with your input and the result added):

```
Enter temperature as Fahrenheit: 80
26 Celsius

Any key to continue...
```

The first two lines come from the *FahrCels* function that is a part of your application. The *menuproc* function adds the "Any key to continue..." message at the bottom of the screen and waits for a keystroke before displaying the menu again.

Pressing **2** displays this message, and everything works the same way:

```
Enter temperature as Celsius: 22
71 Fahrenheit

Any key to continue...
```

The menu continues to display after each selection until you press the **Esc** key, at which point *menuproc* returns and the program terminates.

Data Entry Screens

Exercise 9.1 uses a general-purpose menu manager but otherwise interacts with the user by using conventional standard input and output functions. Interactive programs accept input data from the user in typical ways. Many user interface environments use *dialog boxes* as a consistent and standard way for the user to communicate with the program. As you learned from the Appendix, Quincy, too, uses dialog boxes. The advantages of this approach are that the programmer does not need to rewrite code to do the same job for every program and the user does not need to learn a different interface for different applications.

To illustrate this principle, we will build our own simple data entry screen manager—not quite a dialog box generator, but similar in concept. The program will allow you to describe a data entry template as an array of field definitions. Then, when the program calls the data entry manager function, the function collects the input from the user. To use this facility, an application program includes the **screen.h** header file shown here:

```
#ifndef SCREEN_H
#define SCREEN_H

#include <conio.h>
#include <string.h>
#include <ctype.h>

typedef struct EntryField   {
    char *prompt;
    int x, y;
    int len;
    char *buffer;
} Field;

int DataScreenEntry(char *title, Field *scr);

#endif
```

The **screen.h** header file declares the *Field* structure, which defines the format of a single data entry field. The application program will provide an initialized array of these structures. The format includes a pointer to a string constant that provides prompting text for the user, the screen coordinates and length of the field, and the address of a memory buffer into which the function loads the user's data entry for the field.

The *DataScreenEntry* prototype is for the function that the program calls to collect data values from the user. The first argument points to a string constant for a title for the data entry screen. The second argument points to the array of *Field* structures that describes the data entry template.

Following is the definition of the *DataScreenEntry* function:

```
#include <string.h>
#include <ctype.h>
#include "screen.h"

int DataScreenEntry(char *title, Field *scr)
{
    Field *fld, *end;
    int rtn, done = 0;
    /* --- clear the screen and display the title --- */
    clrscr();
    cursor((80-strlen(title))/2, 0);
    cprintf(title);
```

```
/* --- display the fields and their buffers --- */
for (fld = scr; fld->prompt != NULL; fld++) {
    cursor(fld->x, fld->y);
    cprintf("%s [", fld->prompt);
    cprintf(fld->buffer);
    cursor(fld->x+strlen(fld->prompt)+2+fld->len, fld->y);
    putch(']');
}
end = fld-1;
fld = scr;
/* -- move through the fields, collecting data entries -- */
while (!done)    {
    rtn = DataEntryField(fld);
    switch (rtn)     {
        case DN:                /* down arrow key */
            fld++;
            if (fld->prompt == NULL)
                fld = scr;
            break;
        case UP:                /* up arrow key */
            if (fld-- == scr)
                fld = end;
            break;
        case PGUP:              /* page keys */
        case PGDN:
        case ESC:               /* Esc key */
        case '\r':
            done = 1;
            break;
        default:
            break;
    }
}
return rtn;
}
```

The *DataScreenEntry* function calls the *DataEntryField* function for each entry in the *Field* array. That function is shown here:

```
static int DataEntryField(Field *fld)
{
    int i, key = 0, col = 0, done = 0;
    int x = fld->x+strlen(fld->prompt)+2;
    while (!done)    {
        /* --- position the cursor and read a character --- */
        cursor(x+col, fld->y);
        key = getch();
        switch (key)     {
            case FWD:       /* right arrow key */
                if (col < fld->len)
                    col++;
                break;
```

```
            case BS:        /* left arrow key */
                if (col)
                    --col;
                break;
            case RUBOUT:    /* big left arrow key */
                if (col)
                    cursor(--col+x, fld->y);
            case DEL:         /* Del key */
                if (col < fld->len) {
                    for (i = col; i < fld->len-1; i++)
                        putch(fld->buffer[i]=fld->buffer[i+1]);
                    putch(' ');
                    fld->buffer[i] = '\0';
                }
                break;
            case UP:        /* keys that terminate input */
            case DN:
            case PGUP:
            case PGDN:
            case ESC:
            case '\r':
                done = 1;
                break;
            default:
                if (isprint(key) && col < fld->len) {
                    /* --- data entry key --- */
                    for (i = fld->len-1; i > col; --i)
                        fld->buffer[i] = fld->buffer[i-1];
                    fld->buffer[col] = key;
                    for (i = col; i < fld->len; i++)
                        putch(fld->buffer[i]);
                    col++;
                }
                else
                    putch('\a');
                break;
        }
    }
    return key;
}
```

In a traditional C programming environment, the *DataScreenEntry* and *DataEntryField* functions would be independently compiled and linked with your programs. Quincy has no linker, so the functions are added to the screen.h header file that declares them.

N O T E

Exercise 9.2 uses the menu manager and the data entry screen manager to implement a name and address database.

EXERCISE 9.2 *Data entry screens.*

```c
#include <ctype.h>
#include <stdio.h>
#include <string.h>
#include "menus.h"
#include "screen.h"

/* --- name and address file format --- */
struct Nad {
    char name[21];
    char addr1[26];
    char addr2[26];
    char city[26];
    char state[3];
    char zip[6];
    char phone[16];
} nad;

/* -- data entry template to collect names and addresses -- */
Field scrn[] = {
    {"   Name", 20, 2, sizeof(nad.name)-1,  nad.name},
    {"Address", 20, 3, sizeof(nad.addr1)-1, nad.addr1},
    {"       ", 20, 4, sizeof(nad.addr2)-1, nad.addr2},
    {"   City", 20, 5, sizeof(nad.city)-1,  nad.city},
    {"  State", 20, 6, sizeof(nad.state)-1, nad.state},
    {"    Zip", 20, 7, sizeof(nad.zip)-1,   nad.zip},
    {"  Phone", 20, 8, sizeof(nad.phone)-1, nad.phone},
    {NULL}
};

void AddEntry(void), FindEntry(void);

/* --- menu for adding, retrieving, and changing records --- */
Menu menu[] = {
    {"Add Entry",  AddEntry},
    {"Find Entry", FindEntry},
    {NULL}
};

int main()
{
    menuproc("Names and Addresses", menu);
    return 0;
}
```

continued

```
/* --- add an entry to the data base --- */
void AddEntry(void)
{
    FILE *fp = fopen("nad.dat", "ab");
    if (fp != NULL) {
        memset(&nad, 0, sizeof nad);
        if (DataScreenEntry("Address Book", scrn) == '\r')
            fwrite(&nad, sizeof nad, 1, fp);
        fclose(fp);
    }
}

/* --- find and change an entry in the database --- */
void FindEntry(void)
{
    FILE *fp = fopen("nad.dat", "r+b");
    char sname[6];
    int rtn;
    if (fp != NULL) {
        memset(&nad, 0, sizeof nad);
        /* --- get the name to be found --- */
        if (DataScreenEntry("Address Book", scrn) == '\r') {
            int rcdno = 0;
            strncpy(sname, nad.name, 5);
            sname[5] = '\0';
            memset(&nad, 0, sizeof nad);
            /* --- search the database for the name --- */
            while (strncmp(sname, nad.name, strlen(sname))) {
                if ((rtn = fread(&nad, sizeof nad, 1, fp))==0)
                    break;
                rcdno++;
            }
            if (rtn)    {
                /* --- found the name, get changes --- */
                if (DataScreenEntry("Address Book",scrn)=='\r'){
                    fseek(fp, --rcdno * sizeof nad, SEEK_SET);
                    fwrite(&nad, sizeof nad, 1, fp);
                }
            }
        }
        fclose(fp);
    }
}
```

Exercise 9.2 declares the *Nad* structure, which defines the format of a record in the database. It builds arrays of *Field* and *Menu* structure objects to define the user interface. The *Field* entries include the sizes and addresses of members of the *Nad* structure object. The program includes functions to add, retrieve, and change database records.

When you run Exercise 9.2, it displays this menu on the screen:

```
            Names and Addresses

            1: Add Entry
            2: Find Entry
          Esc: Exit

          Select:
```

To add an entry to the database, press **1**. The program calls the *AddEntry* function, which calls *DataEntryScreen* to display this template and retrieve data values that you enter:

```
                    Address Book

          Name [                    ]
       Address [                      ]
               [                      ]
          City [                      ]
         State [   ]
           Zip [      ]
         Phone [                ]
```

The function uses the information in the *Field* array to construct the template. The title is centered at the top of the screen. The fields are positioned where their definitions specify. The function displays the prompts and adds the square brackets at either end of the data entry areas. Then it moves the cursor to the first position of the first field and waits for some keyboard entry.

You can type characters, use the left and right arrow keys to move the cursor, and use the **Del** and **Rubout** keys to delete letters. The up and down arrow keys move the cursor between fields on the template. As you type data, the program puts it into the buffer pointed to by the *Field* array entry.

When you have completed an entry, you can press **Enter** to add it to the database or **Esc** to ignore it. Pressing one of those keys returns to the *AddEntry* function, which writes the record to the database for the **Enter** key and does not for the **Esc** key. Then the program returns to display the menu again.

To find and possibly change an existing record in the database, press **2** when the menu is displayed. The *FindEntry* function is called and uses the first call to *DataEntryScreen* to get a name to search for in the database. The search uses only the first five characters in the name, so you can type them and press **Enter**. If the program finds a matching entry, it calls *DataEntryScreen* again to display the record and get any changes that you might enter. Once again, press **Enter** to record the changes and **Esc** to reject them.

Exercise 9.2 is not a complete program. You might want to include a delete record function and let the user page forward and backward through the database with the **PgUp** and **PgDn** keys.

Command Line Arguments and Searching File Directories

You used the *argc* and *argv* conventions to process command line arguments in Exercises 5.41 and 7.9. Exercise 9.3 takes that process a step further and shows you how to manage a variable number of command line options that the user can put on the command line in any order. The exercise also introduces Quincy's **dir.h** header file, shown here:

```
#ifndef _DIR_H
#define _DIR_H

struct ffblk {
    char ff_[30];
    char ff_name[13];
};

int findfirst(const char*,struct ffblk*,int);
int findnext(struct ffblk*);

#endif
```

The **dir.h** header declares a structure and functions that let you search a disk directory for files that match a file specification with wild cards. This header file emulates a subset of the same capability that Borland C++ implements.

findfirst

A program declares a *struct ffblk* variable. Then it calls *findfirst,* passing a wild card specification (just like you type for the DOS **DIR** command), the address of the *ffblk* variable, and an attribute value for the file—which, in our example, is always zero.

If a matching file is found, the *findfirst* function returns zero. Otherwise, it returns −1.

findnext

The *findnext* function continues the file search, finding subsequent files that match the wild card criteria. It returns zero as long as files are found, and −1 when no more files are found.

When *findfirst* and *findnext* return, the *struct ffblk* variable has the full, unambiguous name of the current file found in the scan.

Here is an example of how you use these functions:

```
int ax;
struct ffblk ff;

ax = findfirst(*argv, &ff, 0);
while (ax != -1)      {
    FILE *fp = fopen(ff.ff_name, "rt");
    /* process the file ... */
    fclose(fp);
    ax = findnext(&ff);
}
```

Exercise 9.3, shown here, demonstrates command line argument processing and the full use of *findfirst* and *findnext*.

EXERCISE 9.3 *Command line arguments and file scans.*

```
#include <stdio.h>
#include <string.h>
#include <dir.h>

void usage(void);

main(int argc, char *argv[])
{
    FILE *fp;
    char *string, *cp;
    char buf[120];
    int stringlen = 0, buflen, line;
    int ax;
    struct ffblk ff;
```

continued

EXERCISE 9.3 *Command line arguments and file scans (continued).*

```
        char Listonly=0, Linenumbers=0;

        if (argc <= 2)  {
            usage();
            return;
        }

        /* ---- process command line arguments ---- */
        ++argv, -argc;
        while (argc- > 1)  {
            if (**argv == '-')  {   /* command line option flag */
                switch (*(++(*argv))) {
                    case 'l':
                        ++Listonly;
                        break;
                    case 'n':
                        ++Linenumbers;
                        break;
                    default:
                        usage();
                        return;
                }
            }
            else if (stringlen == 0)    {
                string = *argv;
                stringlen = strlen(string);
            }
            else
                usage();
            ++argv;
        }

        /* --- scan files according to file specification --- */
        ax = findfirst(*argv, &ff, 0);
        while (ax != -1)    {
            fp = fopen(ff.ff_name, "rt");
            /* --- read lines of text --- */
            line = 0;
            while ((fgets(buf,sizeof buf,fp)) != NULL)  {
                ++line;
                buflen = strlen(buf);
                /* --- search line for matching pattern --- */
                for (cp = buf; cp+stringlen < buf+buflen; ++cp) {
                    if (!strncmp(cp, string, stringlen))    {
                        /* --- found a match --- */
                        printf("%s", ff.ff_name);
                        if (Listonly) {
```

continued

EXERCISE 9.3 *Command line arguments and file scans (continued).*

```
                              /* --- listing files only --- */
                              putchar('\n');
                              goto breakout;
                    }
                    if (Linenumbers)
                              /* --- printing file numbers --- */
                              printf(" %5d", line);
                    putchar(':');
                    /* --- display matching line --- */
                    fputs(buf, stdout);
                    break;
                }
            }
        }
breakout:
        fclose(fp);
        ax = findnext(&ff);
    }
}

/* --- explain usage to the user --- */
void usage(void)
{
    fprintf(stderr, "\nUsage: [-l] [-n] <pattern> <file>");
    fprintf(stderr, "\n\t-l    list file names only");
    fprintf(stderr, "\n\t-n    print line numbers");
}
```

Exercise 9.3 is a program that searches one or more text files for lines of text with strings that match an argument. For example, if you wanted to find in a number of programs all the text lines that reference a particular identifier, this program could find them for you. The command line format is as follows:

```
 [-l] [-n] <pattern> <file>
```

The square brackets mean that the command line switch is optional. The –l option means that you want to list the names of the files that have matching strings but that you do not want to display the matching strings. The –n option means that when you display matching strings, you want to display the line number, too.

Suppose, for example, that you want to find and view all the lines of code where the exercise programs in this chapter reference the *putch* or *putchar* functions. Set the command line option in Quincy to this value:

```
-n putch ex09*.c
```

You can put the options in any sequence as long as the file specification comes last. When you run the program, you see this display:

```
EX09003.C    66:   putchar('\n');
EX09003.C    72:   putchar(':');
EX09004.C   102:   putch(BELL);
EX09004.C   172:   putch(mark);
```

To view only the file names, use the –l option. When the program finds the first occurrence of the search string, it stops scanning that file and proceeds to the next one.

Exercise 9.3 demonstrates what is probably the only begrudgingly sanctioned use of the infamous *goto* statement, which is to break out of multiple inner loops with one statement. The program could have avoided that usage and preserved its structured integrity by setting a flag and testing it at the bottom of each inner loop to see whether it needed to break out. I'll leave it to you to decide which idiom you prefer.

Tic-Tac-Toe: A Board Game

Exercise 9.4 is a tic-tac-toe game. You play against the computer. You always move first. The exercise uses many of the C language techniques that you have learned. It uses the **conio.h** functions to read and write the console. It uses string constants with hexadecimal escape sequences that represent characters from the PC's extended graphics character set. These characters are used to display the game's nine-element matrix. A two-dimensional array defines the row, column, and diagonal game vectors that constitute a win.

EXERCISE 9.4 *Tic-tac-toe.*

```c
#include <conio.h>
#include <string.h>

/*                        */
/* A simple game of tic-tac-toe */
/*                        */
#define TRUE 1
#define FALSE 0
#define BELL 7
/* ---- board markers ---- */
#define PLAYER 'X'
#define COMPUTER 'O'
#define FREE ' '
/* --- game position on screen --- */
#define LEFT 10
#define TOP   5
/* --- game board --- */
static char board[9];
/* --- winning combinations --- */
static int wins [8][3] = {
    1,2,3, 4,5,6, 7,8,9,    /* winning rows     */
    1,4,7, 2,5,8, 3,6,9,    /* winning columns  */
    1,5,9, 3,5,7            /* winning diagonals */
};
/* -------- prototypes --------- */
void nextmove(void), displayboard(void), setpiece(int, int);
void message(int, char*);
int getmove(void), won(void), canwin(int), trywin(int,int *);

int main()
{
    int mv, i;
    int moves;
    int ch = 'y';
    while (ch == 'y')   {
        memset(board, FREE, 9);
        displayboard();
        /* --- get player's first move --- */
        if ((mv = getmove()) == 0)
            break;
        /* --- set computer's first move --- */
        if (mv != 5)
            setpiece(5, COMPUTER);  /* center if available  */
        else
            setpiece(1, COMPUTER);  /* upper left otherwise */
```

continued

EXERCISE 9.4 *Tic-tac-toe (continued).*

```
        moves = 2;
        while (moves < 9) {
            getmove();              /* player's next move */
            moves++;
            if (won())  {
                message(1, "You win");
                break;
            }
            if (moves == 9)
                message(1, "Tie");
            else    {
                /* --- find computer's next move --- */
                if ((mv = canwin(COMPUTER)) != 0)
                    /* --- win if possible --- */
                    setpiece(mv, COMPUTER);
                else if ((mv = canwin(PLAYER)) != 0)
                    /* --- block player's win potential --- */
                    setpiece(mv, COMPUTER);
                else
                    nextmove();
                if (won())  {
                    message(1, "I win");
                    break;
                }
                moves++;
            }
        }
        message(2, "Play again? (y/n) ");
        ch = getch();
    }
    return 0;
}
/* --- find computer's next move --- */
void nextmove(void)
{
    int i;

    for (i = 0; i < 9; i++) {
        if (board[i] == FREE) {
            setpiece(i+1, COMPUTER);
            break;
        }
    }
}
```

continued

EXERCISE 9.4 *Tic-tac-toe (continued).*

```
/* --- get the player's move and post it --- */
int getmove(void)
{
    int mv = 0;

    while (mv == 0) {
        message(0, "Move (1-9)? ");
        mv = getch();
        mv -= '0';
        if (mv < 1 || mv > 9 || board[mv-1] != FREE)    {
            putch(BELL);
            mv = 0;
        }
    }
    setpiece(mv, PLAYER);
    return mv;
}

/* ------ test to see if the game has been won ------- */
int won(void)
{
    int i, k;
    for (i = 0; i < 8; i++) {
        if (board[wins[i][0]-1] == FREE)
            continue;
        for (k = 1; k < 3; k++)
            if (board[wins[i][0]-1] != board[wins[i][k]-1])
                break;
        if (k == 3)
            return TRUE;
    }
    return FALSE;
}
/* --- test to see if a player (n) can win this time --- */
int canwin(int n)
{
    int i, w;

    for (i = 0; i < 8; i++)
        if ((w = trywin(n, wins[i])) != 0)
            return w;
    return 0;
}
```

continued

EXERCISE 9.4 *Tic-tac-toe continued.*

```
/* ---- test a row, column, or diagonal for a win ---- */
int trywin(int n,int *wn)
{
    int nct = 0, zct = 0, i;

    for (i = 0; i < 3; i++)
        if (board[*(wn + i)-1] == FREE)
            zct = i+1;
        else if (board[*(wn + i)-1] == n)
            nct++;
    if (nct == 2 && zct)
        return *(wn + zct - 1);
    return 0;
}
/* ------ display the tic-tac-toe board ------ */
void displayboard(void)
{
    int y;
    static char ln1[] = "   \xb3   \xb3";
    static char ln2[] =
        "\xc4\xc4\xc4\xc5\xc4\xc4\xc4\xc5\xc4\xc4\xc4";
    clrscr();
    for (y = 0; y < 5; y++) {
        cursor(LEFT,TOP+y);
        cprintf((y&1) ? ln2 : ln1);
    }
}
/* ---- set a players mark (O or X) on the board ---- */
void setpiece(int pos, int mark)
{
    int row, col;
    board[-pos] = mark;

    col = pos / 3;
    row = pos % 3;
    cursor(LEFT+row*4+1, TOP+col*2);
    putch(mark);
}
/* ---- message to opponent ---- */
void message(int y, char *m)
{
    cursor(LEFT, TOP+8+y);
    cprintf(m);
}
```

Enjoy playing the game, and use its code to see how such programs are written. As an exercise, modify the program so that the human player and the computer alternate going first.

It is possible to beat the computer. Figure out how and then modify the program to make it less possible.

N O T E

Summary

This chapter brings together many of the things that you learned in this book, and it brings to a close these tutorial sessions that we have shared. Now you are prepared to find your place among the many productive C programmers in the computer industry. You can continue to use Quincy as a learning tool and to experiment. You can use it as a prototyping tool to check out small functions to add to a bigger system. But Quincy has done its job. It has provided a vehicle with which you learned C. You are ready for bigger things now. You can get a full compiler system—from one of many vendors—that runs on the PC, Amiga, Macintosh, PowerPC, or whatever computer you use, under DOS, Windows, OS/2, NT, UNIX, or whatever operating system you use. You can explore the many commercial and shareware function libraries that support database management, accounting, user interfaces, communications, math functions, graphics, design, and any of hundreds of custom problem domains. In short, you are ready to be a C programmer.

Appendix

QUINCY USER'S GUIDE

*T*his Appendix describes Quincy, the C language interpreter with which you view and run the exercises in this book. You can also use Quincy to develop, test, and modify other small C language programs.

Introduction to Quincy

Quincy is a C language interpreter similar in operation to the MS-DOS QBasic interpreter except that Quincy implements standard C instead of BASIC.

Quincy was originally developed by programmer Bob Brodt as a shareware command line program called the Small C Interpreter. SCI implemented a small subset of K&R C. Later, Bob and I enhanced SCI with more C features, integrated it with a full-screen source code editor and debugger, renamed it Quincy (after my daughter's cat), and released it commercially. A few copies still sell, and the profits go to charity through an agreement that Bob and I made.

When I undertook the writing of this book, I wanted to include a free compiler on the companion diskette, one that could be integrated with the tutorial to run the exercises. Over the years I had played with Quincy in my spare time, adding ANSI C features mainly as an exercise to better understand the C language. Quincy was, therefore, a good choice for this book. I changed the user interface, installing one that loosely complies with the Common User Access (CUA) interface standard now prevalent in DOS, Windows, and OS/2 applications. Then I built an on-line tutorial from the Help engine of the user interface library and integrated it with the interpreter.

Support for Quincy

The companion diskette that accompanies this book has the most recent version of Quincy at the time the book went to press. As I release newer versions, I make them available for no charge from the CompuServe Information Service. Sign onto the service and log onto the public DDJ forum, which supports readers of *Dr. Dobb's Journal*. Quincy is available for download from the libraries there. You need the PKUNZIP utility program to decompress the file.

You can download the source code for Quincy as well. You will also need D-Flat, the user interface function library that Quincy uses. Search the forum library with the keywords QUINCY and DFLAT to get the latest versions. You need Borland C++ 3.1 or later to compile Quincy.

For help with Quincy or to ask questions about C or this book, send me a message on the public DDJ forum. My CIS Userid is 71101,1262. You can send electronic mail through the Internet by using the CompuServe gateway. My

Internet address is 71101.1262@compuServe.com. Please do not send large unsolicited files of your source code for me to look at. I make this request because readers often do just that, and I rarely have time to look at large segments of their work. Send snippets of code that describe the situation. We can discuss the problem first. Then if I need to see more code, I'll ask for it.

A CompuServe account is as essential to a programmer as any other tool. The technical support available there is superior to any that you can get from software vendors, even when you pay for it. Most vendors have forums where you can ask questions. If their staff can't answer a question, chances are that another user who sees your message can. Many helpful experts in many fields monitor the technical forums daily.

The Quincy C Language Implementation

Quincy runs programs that are fully contained within one translation unit in the language of the ANSI standard C definition document. That means that all the source code is contained in one file along with the header files that the principal file includes. There is no link process that joins independently compiled translation units into an executable module.

Quincy is an interpreter. It uses a lexical scan to translate the C language source code into tokens. It interprets the tokens to run the program. Some of traditional C's compile-time error checking occurs at run-time under Quincy. Other error checking occurs during the lexical scan.

Quincy implements most of Standard C. Arrays are limited to four dimensions. Bitmap structure members are not supported. Not all of the standard library functions are included. Quincy provides no support for the functions and other declarations in **signal.h**, **locale.h**, **limits.h**, or **float.h**. The other standard headers are supported but with a subset of their full capabilities.

Preprocessor

Quincy includes a preprocessor and supports the following listed preprocessing tokens:

```
#define
#elif
#else
```

```
#endif
#if
#ifdef
#ifndef
#include
#undef
```

Standard Libraries

Quincy includes the following listed standard C header files and implements the listed subset of the standard C library data structures, functions, and macros:

ASSERT.H	log	fprintf
assert	log10	fputc
CTYPE.H	pow	fputs
isalnum	sin	fread
isalpha	sinh	fscanf
isdigit	sqrt	fseek
islower	tan	ftell
isprint	tanh	fwrite
isspace	SETJMP.H	getc
isupper	jmp_buf	getchar
tolower	longjmp	gets
toupper	setjmp	NULL
ERRNO.H	STDARG.H	printf
errno	va_arg	putc
MATH.H	va_end	putchar
acos	va_list	puts
asin	va_start	remove
atan	STDIO.H	rename
atan2	EOF	rewind
ceil	fclose	scanf
cos	fflush	SEEK_CUR
cosh	fgetc	SEEK_END
exp	fgets	SEEK_SET
fabs	FILE	sprintf
floor	fopen	sscanf

stdaux	calloc	strncmp
stderr	exit	strncpy
stdin	free	TIME.H
stdout	malloc	asctime
stdprn	rand	ctime
tmpfile	srand	difftime
tmpnam	system	gmtime
ungetc	STRING.H	localtime
STDLIB.H	memset	mktime
abort	strcat	struct tm
abs	strcmp	time
atof	strcpy	time_t
atoi	strlen	
atol	strncat	

Nonstandard Libraries

Quincy includes the following nonstandard header files with the functions listed:

CONIO.H	cursor	DIR.H
clrscr	getch	findfirst
cprintf	putch	findnext

Installing Quincy

The companion diskette includes these files:

```
QNC.EXE        Quincy's executable program
QUINCY.HLP     The Quincy Help database
TUTORIAL.HLP   The Tutorial Help database
ASSERT.H       Library header file
CONIO.H          "        "        "
CTYPE.H          "        "        "
DIR.H            "        "        "
ERRNO.H          "        "        "
MATH.H           "        "        "
```

```
SETJMP.H        Library header file
STDARG.H          "       "        "
STDIO.H           "       "        "
STDLIB.H          "       "        "
STRING.H          "       "        "
TIME.H            "       "        "
EXnnxxx.C       Exercise source code (nn = chapter, xxx =
                                     exercise number)
MENUS.H           "       "        "   (Chapter 9)
SCREEN.H          "       "        "   (     "     )
EMPLOYEE.H        "       "        "   (     "     )
```

You can install everything in one subdirectory, or you can install Quincy's files in one subdirectory and the exercise source code files in another. To install the files, copy them from the distribution medium to the subdirectories on your computer's disk.

Installation Requirements

You need an IBM PC–compatible computer with at least 640K of memory and MS-DOS 3.3 or greater. You can run Quincy from diskettes, but it runs much better from a hard drive. Quincy uses the mouse if you have one installed, but you can operate everything by using the keyboard.

Running Quincy

You can start Quincy alone or by specifying the name of a text file on the command line:

```
C>qnc test.c
```

If you start it alone, you see the screen shown in Figure A.1.

Quincy's screen is divided into the areas shown in Figure A.1. At the top is the *title bar*, which identifies Quincy's version and the name of the program loaded, if any. The *menu bar* is just below the title bar. It contains the labels for Quincy's *pull-down menus*. Most of the screen is occupied by the *text editor window*. That is where you view and modify a program's source code. If a mouse is installed, the right side and bottom of the editor window have *scroll bars* with *scroll buttons* at either end and a sliding *scroll box* in the scroll bar. They work with the mouse to scroll and page through the program. The bottom line is the *status bar*. It tells you the time and date in the right corner and the current program line and column number in the middle.

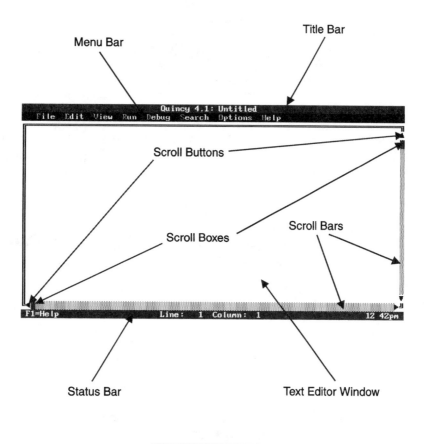

FIGURE A.1 *The Quincy screen.*

Menus

Quincy has eight pull-down menus. You pull a menu down by clicking its label in the menu bar or by holding the **Alt** key down and pressing the first letter of the menu label. For example, **Alt+F** pops down the File menu, which Figure A.2 shows.

FIGURE A.2 *The File menu.*

When a menu is pulled down, you can make a selection from the menu by clicking its label, by using the arrow keys to move the highlight bar to the label and pressing **Enter**, or by pressing the shortcut key that is highlighted in the selection's label.

Some menu selections have *accelerator* keys. For example, the Exit selection on the File menu has **Alt+X** as its accelerator key. You can execute a menu selection without pulling down the menu by pressing the accelerator key while you are editing or debugging a program.

Dialog Boxes

You enter data into or select choices from dialog boxes to provide information for Quincy to operate on. Figure A.3 is the File Open dialog box that you use to select program files to load into Quincy.

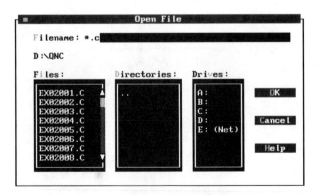

FIGURE A.3 *The File Open dialog box.*

Dialog boxes have text entry controls, checkboxes, radio buttons, listboxes, and command buttons. You can move from control to control by clicking a control with the mouse, by tabbing to the next control, or by pressing **Alt+** the control's shortcut key, which is highlighted in the text label associated with the control.

Most dialog boxes have one or more standard command buttons. They are labeled **OK**, **Cancel**, and **Help**. Choose **OK** to use the values in the dialog box and return to the editor/debugger. Choose **Cancel** to ignore the dialog box values and return to the editor/debugger without making any selections. Choose **Help** to read a help text window about the dialog box.

The **Enter** key chooses the **OK** command button in most cases. The **Esc** key chooses the **Cancel** button. The **F1** function key chooses the **Help** command button.

Writing a New Program

You can begin typing a program into Quincy as soon as you start it. If you are looking at a different text file and want to begin typing a new one, choose the **New** command on the File menu. This action clears the edit buffer and lets you begin typing a new file. If you have made changes to the prior file without saving it, Quincy asks whether you want to save the file. The next section explains how you save a new file.

Loading and Saving a Program's Source Code

To load a program into Quincy, choose the **Open** command on the File menu. Quincy displays the File Open dialog box shown in Figure A.3. You can type a fully qualified file path and name into the **Filename** field and choose **OK**, or you can use the Files, Directories, and Drives listboxes to navigate the computer's file system and find a file. If you type a file name with DOS wild cards, the dialog box displays the files in the Files listbox that match that specification. When the **Filename** field has a complete file name, choosing **OK** closes the dialog box and loads that file into the editor.

Editing the Program

Type changes to the program at any time. Table A.1 summarizes the keystrokes for editing text and moving the cursor.

TABLE A.1 *Source code editing keys.*

KEY	ACTION
F3	Next search.
Arrow keys	Move the cursor one character.
Ctrl+arrow	Move the cursor one word.
Shift+arrow	Mark a block.
Del	Delete character to the right of the cursor. If a block is marked, delete the block.
Backspace	Delete character to the left of the cursor. If a block is marked, delete the block.
PgUp (PgDn)	Scroll forward (back) one page.
Ctrl+PgUp (PgDn)	Scroll horizontally one page.
Shift+PgUp (PgDn)	Mark a block.
Home (End)	Move the cursor to the beginning (end) of the line.
Ctrl+Home (End)	Move the cursor to the beginning (end) of the document.
Shift+Home (End)	Mark a block.
Tab	Tab to the next Tab Stop position.

Using the Mouse

You can use the mouse for moving the keyboard cursor, marking text blocks, and paging and scrolling text. Marked blocks are used for clipboard operations, described next. The scroll bars and buttons facilitate moving around the text file with the mouse.

To set the keyboard cursor with the mouse, move the mouse cursor to the character to select and click the left button.

To page forward and backward with the mouse, click on the scroll bar to one side or the other of the scroll box. You can click on the scroll box and drag it to another position in the scroll bar to move to that relative location of the text file in the window. You can scroll a line or column at a time by clicking the scroll button at either end of the scroll bar.

Mark a block of text with the mouse by clicking at one end of the block, holding the mouse button down, and dragging the mouse to the other end. The block of text is highlighted, as shown in Figure A.4.

```
                        Quincy 4.1: EX06003.C
        File  Edit  View  Run  Debug  Search  Options  Help

int main()
{
    int ans = -1;
    while (ans != 0)     {
        /* --- mark the top of the parsing descent --- */
        if (setjmp(errjb) == 0) {
            pos = 0;     /* initialize string subscript */
            /* ---- read an expression ----- */
            puts("\nEnter expression (0 to quit): ");
            gets(expr);
            /* --- evaluate the expression --- */
            ans = addsubt();
            if (expr[pos] != '\0')
                error();
            printf("%d", ans);
        }
        else
            /* --- an error occurred --- */
            printf("\nTry again");

F1=Help                    Line:  35  Column:  1                    6 08pm
```

FIGURE A.4 *A marked block of text.*

Using the Clipboard

You can *cut* and *copy* marked blocks of text to the *Clipboard*, an internal text buffer, by choosing the **Cut** and **Copy** commands on the Edit menu. The **Cut** command deletes the text from its marked position. The **Copy** command leaves the marked text intact.

When there is text in the Clipboard, you can *paste* the text into the text file at the current cursor position by choosing the **Paste** command on the Edit menu.

Search and Replace Text

To find a specified string of text in the source code file, choose the **Search** command on the Search menu. It displays the Search Text dialog box shown in Figure A.5.

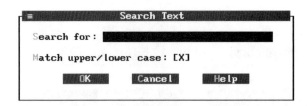

FIGURE A.5 *The Search Text dialog box.*

Type a text string into the **Search for** field. Set the **Match upper/lower case** checkbox according to what you want. Choose **OK**. The program searches from the current cursor position forward to the end of the file. If the text string is found, the program highlights the matching text in the editor window and moves the cursor to it. If the string is not found, a message is displayed.

To replace a specified string of text in the source code with another string, choose the **Replace** command on the Search menu. It displays the Replace Text dialog box shown in Figure A.6.

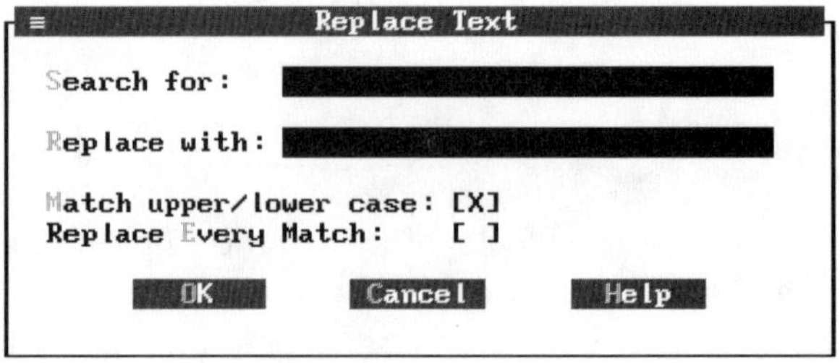

FIGURE A.6 *The Replace Text dialog box.*

Type a text string into the **Search for** field and another into the **Replace with** field. Set the **Match upper/lower case** and **Replace Every Match** checkboxes according to what you want. Choose **OK**. The program searches from the current cursor position forward to the end of the file. If the text string is found, the program replaces the matching text in the editor window and moves the cursor to it. If not, a message is displayed.

Printing the Program's Source Code

To print the program's source code, choose the **Print** command on the File menu. Make sure that the printer is connected, turned on, on line, and loaded with paper.

Choosing a Printer Port

The **Print** command uses LPT1 by default. If your printer is connected to a different port, choose the **Printer Setup** command on the File menu. The program displays the Printer Setup dialog box shown in Figure A.7.

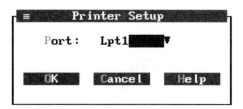

FIGURE A.7 *The Printer Setup dialog box.*

You can type in a printer port or press the down arrow key to pop down the listbox with valid printer ports to select from. Select one and choose **OK**.

Running a Program

Run the C program by choosing the **Run** command on the Run menu. Observe that **F9** is the accelerator key to run a program. You can press **F9** to run the program without selecting the menu. Quincy clears the screen and starts the program. While the program is running, the screen is used for standard output (unless standard output is redirected). When the program is finished running, it displays this message at the bottom of the screen:

```
Press any key to return to Quincy...
```

Press a key to return to Quincy's editor/debugger window.

Command-Line Options

You can set command line options for the program to use with its *main(int argc, char *argv[])* convention. Choose the **Command Line** command on the Options menu. Quincy displays the dialog box shown in Figure A.8.

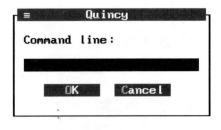

FIGURE A.8 *The Command Line Input dialog box.*

Enter the command line options just as you would enter them on the DOS command line after the program name. Choose **OK**. All subsequent program executions use these command line options until you change them or exit from and rerun Quincy.

Input/Output Redirection

You can set input/output redirection commands in the Command Line dialog box. Put the **<** and **>** tokens and the file names on the command line entry field just as you would put them on the DOS command line.

Memory Options

The **Memory** command on the Options menu opens the Memory Options dialog box shown in Figure A.9.

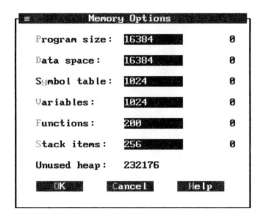

FIGURE A.9 *The Memory Options dialog box.*

This dialog box allows you to specify Quincy's internal table sizes. In most cases, the default values suffice, but if you find that you are out of memory when trying to run programs, you can change some of the memory allocations.

PROGRAM SIZE

The **Program size** field specifies the number of bytes allocated to a compiled program. This is not the size of the source code; rather, it is the size of the tokenized program after preprocessing and the lexical scan.

DATA SPACE

The **Data space** field specifies in bytes how much space is available for global and local variables. A program's requirements depend on how many variables can be in scope at any one time.

SYMBOL TABLE

The **Symbol table** field specifies the maximum number of unique identifiers the program may declare. This table has nothing to do with scope. It is just a table of logical symbols that have been reduced to integer values.

VARIABLES

The **Variables** field specifies how many variables the program may declare. Quincy builds a table of variables with an entry for each unique global and local declaration. There is one table per variable regardless of how many times the variable is currently instantiated.

FUNCTIONS

The **Functions** field specifies the maximum number of functions the program may declare. This number includes standard library functions.

STACK ITEMS

The **Stack items** field specifies the maximum number of items that may be on the expression analyzer stack. Note that this stack is not like the stack in a conventional compiled program. This stack holds variable table entries for the interim results of expressions that are being evaluated and arguments that are being passed to functions.

UNUSED HEAP

You do not change the **Unused heap** field. It tells you how much heap space is available from the system for Quincy to use. Quincy responds to a program's calls to *malloc* and *calloc* by allocating memory from the system heap.

Debugging

Quincy has a built-in source-level debugger. It integrates the editor and debugger in one environment. You can step through programs, examine and modify variables, set breakpoints and watches, and view the function execution history.

Single Stepping

Press **F7** or choose the **Step** command on the Run menu to step through the program one source code line at a time. Quincy displays the next source code line to be executed with a highlighted bar, as shown in Figure A.10.

```
                           Quincy 4.1: TTT.C
    File   Edit   View   Run   Debug   Search   Options   Help
/* --------- prototypes ----------- */
void nextmove(void), showgame(void);
int getmove(void), won(void), canwin(int), trywin(int,int *);

int main()
{
    int mv, i;
    int moves = 2;
    showgame();
    mv = getmove();
    if (mv != 4)
        bd[4] = COMPUTER;
    else
        bd[0] = COMPUTER;
    showgame();
    while (moves < 9) {
        getmove();
        if (won())  {
            showgame();
            printf("\nYou win!");

 F1=Help                        Line:  33  Column:  1                6:23pm
```

FIGURE A.10 *Stepping through a program.*

If a line of code involves standard input or output, Quincy switches to the output screen display momentarily when you step through the source code line.

Functions defined in header files are not stepped through. Quincy steps over them. If you need to debug such a function, move it into the main source code file.

Stepping over Functions

Press **F8** or choose the **Step Over** command on the Run menu to execute a function without stepping through its code.

Nonstop Run

At any time during stepping, you can tell the program to resume running by pressing **F9** or choosing the **Run** command on the Run menu.

Interrupting the Program

While the program is running, you can interrupt it by pressing **Ctrl+Break** or **Ctrl+C**. Quincy stops the program at the current source code line and goes into step mode. This procedure allows you to break out of dead loops and step through the code from the point of the interruption.

Examining and Modifying Variables

To examine the value of a variable, choose the **Examine** command on the View menu. This action opens the Examine dialog box shown in Figure A.11.

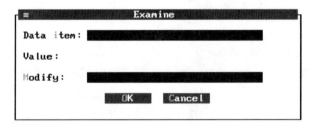

FIGURE A.11 *The Examine dialog box.*

Enter the name of the variable—along with pointer dereferencing and subscripts, if appropriate—and choose **OK**. The current value of the variable is shown in the read-only **Value** field, and the cursor moves to the **Modify** field. To change the variable, enter a new value and choose **OK**. The debugger returns to the environment so that you can continue stepping through the program.

Watching Variables

To maintain a continuous watch of a variable, press **Alt+W** or choose **Add a Watch Variable** on the Debug menu. This action displays the dialog box shown in Figure A.12.

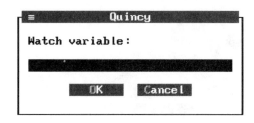

FIGURE A.12 *The Watch dialog box.*

Enter the name of the variable to watch and choose **OK**. Quincy opens the Watch Window at the bottom of the screen with the variable's name and current value, as shown in Figure A.13.

```
                        Quincy 4.1: EX04012.C
    File   Edit   View   Run   Debug   Search   Options   Help
 /* ---- ex04012.c ---- */
 #include <stdio.h>
 #include <stdlib.h>

 int main()
 {
     char sel = '\0';
     while (sel != 'q')  {
         printf("\nS-how number, Q-uit: ");
         sel = getchar();
         fflush(stdin);
         if (sel != 's' && sel != 'q')   {
             putchar('\a');
             continue;
         }
         if (sel == 's')

                         Watch Variables
 char sel='s'

 F1=Help                 Line:  11  Column:  1                6 28pm
```

FIGURE A.13 *The Watch window.*

As you step through the program, the value of the watched variable changes in the Watch Window when the program modifies the variable. When a watched variable goes out of scope, the value shown is "??".

Viewing Functions

You can view a list of all the functions in a running program and a list of the function history by choosing the **Functions** and **Function History** commands on the View menu. Both commands display the dialog box—but with different titles—shown in Figure A.14.

FIGURE A.14 *Function lists.*

The Function List display is a list of all the nonlibrary functions in the program. The Function History display shows the current function running, followed by the function that called the current function, and so on to the bottom of the history, which lists *main* as the first function executed.

These lists are available only when the program is running. You can select one of the functions in the list, and Quincy moves its editor cursor to that function. This selection does not change the current execution position in the running program.

Breakpoints

To set a breakpoint on or off, position the keyboard cursor on a line of code and press **F2** or choose the **Breakpoint On/Off** command on the Debug menu. Quincy highlights the breakpoint line in the display. Breakpoints take effect when you run a program rather than step through it. When the program reaches the line of code where the breakpoint occurs, Quincy interrupts the program and enters the editor/debugger with the breakpoint line selected as the current line in step execution mode.

Clear all breakpoints by choosing the **Delete All Breakpoints** command on the Debug menu.

Changing Quincy's Display Options

Quincy defaults to the screen size currently in effect when you run it. If you are using a color monitor, Quincy defaults to a color window display. If you have a mouse installed, Quincy puts scroll bars on the editor window by default. You can override these defaults by choosing the **Display** command on the Options menu, which displays the Display dialog box shown in Figure A.15.

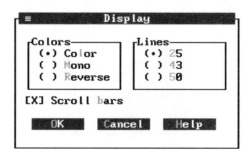

FIGURE A.15 *The Display dialog box.*

Color

The screen colors can be Quincy's default color configuration, a monochrome configuration, or a reverse monochrome configuration that works best on some laptop liquid crystal displays. If your computer uses a Monochrome Display Adapter or equivalent, Quincy uses the monochrome configuration by default.

Screen Size

Quincy uses the current screen character size on startup unless you change it by choosing one of the three selections in the **Lines** field. Only the selections that work with your video system are displayed.

Scroll Bars

If there is a mouse, you get scroll bars by default. If not, you don't. To override the default, set the **Scroll Bars** checkbox accordingly.

Tab Settings

Quincy's default tab settings for source code are one tab every four character positions. You can select two, four, six, or eight tab stops by choosing the **Tabs** command on the Options menu. This action pops down the cascaded Tabs menu shown in Figure A.16.

FIGURE A.16 *The Tabs menu.*

Choose any of the tab position selections on the menu, and the display adjusts itself accordingly. This change affects only those source code files that have tab characters in their text. It does not change files that use space characters for indenting.

Running the DOS Command Shell

You can run DOS from Quincy by choosing the **DOS** command on the File menu. Quincy shells out to DOS and displays this message on the screen:

```
To return to Quincy, execute the DOS exit command.

Microsoft(R) MS-DOS(R) Version 6.20
            (C)Copyright Microsoft Corp 1981-1993.
```

The DOS version message reflects the version of DOS that you are running. This message is followed by the DOS prompt. Execute the DOS commands you need and then execute the **EXIT** command to return to Quincy. Be aware that memory is limited during a shelled-out DOS session. Quincy is still in memory, and so is an additional copy of the command shell program that Quincy loads to service your DOS commands.

Quincy's Help System

Quincy features an on-line, context-sensitive help system. Most dialog boxes have a **Help** command button that loads a help window to explain the dialog box and its controls. You can press **F1** from almost anywhere in Quincy and get a help window that explains the current context.

If the editor cursor is positioned on a C language key word, standard library function, or standard library header file name, **F1** opens a window that explains that part of the C language. You can also double-click the mouse on those text items to open their help windows.

The Help menu includes a **Help for help** command that explains how the help system works, a **Keys help** command that summarizes Quincy's keystrokes, a **Help index** command that displays a list of help topics that you can view, an **About** command that shows Quincy's logo and copyright notice, and a **Tutorial** command, described next.

Running the C Language Tutorial

When used in conjunction with this book, the Quincy C language tutorial can speed up the learning process. To use it, you must first choose the **Tutorial** command on the Help menu, which pops up the cascaded Tutorial menu shown in Figure A.17.

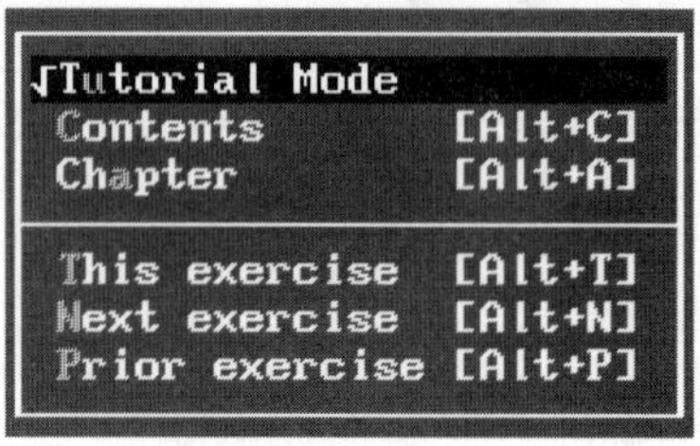

```
√Tutorial Mode
 Contents       [Alt+C]
 Chapter        [Alt+A]

 This exercise  [Alt+T]
 Next exercise  [Alt+N]
 Prior exercise [Alt+P]
```

FIGURE A.17 *The Tutorial menu.*

Initially, the only active command on the menu is the **Tutorial Mode** command. This command toggles the tutorial mode, which is off by default. When you turn it on, Quincy displays a help window with the chapters of the book listed. You can choose one of these by tabbing to it and pressing **Enter** or by double-clicking it. This action displays a list of the exercises in the chapter. You can choose one of these in the same way, usually beginning with the first one.

Choosing an exercise loads its source code into the editor and displays a help window that gives the corresponding page number in this book and briefly lists the object lesson being addressed. The tutorial opens the Watch Window and adds variables to it that are of interest when you run the exercise program.

To run the exercise, press **Esc** to close the help window and proceed with the program. You can use the keys and commands listed in Table A.2 to navigate through the tutorial.

TABLE A.2 *Tutorial commands.*

KEY	TUTORIAL MENU COMMAND	DISPLAYS
Alt+C	Contents	Table of contents
Alt+A	Chapter	Current chapter's exercise list
Alt+T	This Exercise	Current exercise's help window
Alt+N	Next Exercise	Next exercise in the chapter
Alt+P	Prior Exercise	Previous exercise in the chapter

Exiting from Quincy

Exit from Quincy by pressing **Alt+X** or by choosing the **Exit** command from the File menu. If you have made changes to the program and have not saved them, Quincy displays a message that asks whether you want to save the changed source code before exiting.

Glossary

A

Address

An expression that returns the memory address of a variable or function.

Algorithm

The formula or procedure by which a set of program instructions performs a defined task.

Application

A program or group of programs that combine to support a defined user-related function, such as payroll, inventory, accounting, and so on.

Applications program

As opposed to "systems program." A program that is developed for a specific purpose within an application.

Argument

The value passed to a function or subroutine. Its type must match that of the corresponding parameter in the declaration. See "parameter."

Array

A group of variables of the same type organized into a table of one or more dimensions.

ASCII

American Standard Code for Information Exchange. The 8-bit system for encoding digits, the alphabet, special characters, graphics characters, and certain control values.

Assignment

A statement that places the value of an expression into a memory variable.

Associativity

The order in which operands in an expression are evaluated—left-to-right or right-to-left. Associativity is determined by the operator.

Automatic variable

A local variable that does not retain its value when it goes out of scope. Each recursive execution of functions has its own copy of automatic variables.

Binary operator

An operator, such as +, that has two operands.

Boolean logic

The system of logic that applies the AND, OR, and XOR operators to two bitwise operands.

Breakpoint

A debugging procedure in which the program's execution is stopped at a specified statement in the source code so that the programmer can examine the program's state.

Byte

An 8-bit quantity used to store a character value or an integer in the signed range −128 to 127 or unsigned range 0 to 255.

Cast

A parenthesized expression having only a type. It tells the compiler to convert the expression that follows to the type in the parentheses. Also called a *typecast*.

Character

An 8-bit value that represents one of the units in the computer's character set.

Code

Computer instructions encoded in machine, assembly, or high-level language. To write code.

Comment

An informational statement in a program. The comment provides program documentation for the reader of the code. It reserves no memory and has no effect on the program's execution. Comments begin with /* characters and end with */ characters. They may span several lines, and they do not nest.

Compiler

A program that reads high-level language source code and generates object code.

Condition

An expression that returns a true or a false value.

Console

The computer's keyboard and screen.

Constant

A memory object with a defined value that cannot be changed while the program is running.

Control structures

The building blocks of structured programming: sequence, selection, and iteration. The sequence control structure is the sequential expression of imperative statements. The selection control structure is the *if-then-else* decision process. The iteration control structure is the *while-until* loop mechanism. Others are the *for* iteration and the *switch-case* selection control structures.

Cursor

A screen pointer that tells the user where the next keystroke will be echoed. When the system uses a mouse, an additional cursor points to the current mouse position.

Database

A collection of data files loosely integrated to support a common application.

Debugger

A systems program that helps a programmer debug an applications program. The debugger traces the program's source code and supports breakpoints, watchpoints, and the examination and modification of memory variables.

Decision

The process whereby a program alters the statement execution sequence by testing a condition.

Declaration

The program statement that associates an identifier with what it identifies. A declaration can declare a variable, specify the format of a structure, declare an external variable, or declare a function or subroutine's return value and parameter list. A declaration may or may not reserve memory.

Definition

The program statement that defines the existence of a variable or function. A definition reserves memory for the item. The definition sometimes doubles as the item's declaration.

Dimension

The number of elements in an array. When the array is multidimensional—as in an array of arrays—the secondary dimension is the number of array elements in the array.

DOS

The dominant disk operating system for PCs. Also called PC-DOS and MS-DOS. Other operating systems are OS/2, Unix, and Windows NT.

E

Editor

A utility program with which a programmer creates and modifies source code and other text files.

Element

One entry in an array of variables.

Error message

A message that a program displays to tell the user that an error has occurred in the processing.

Escape sequence

Two-character combinations coded into string and character constants that begin with a backslash character and compile to a one-character value that usually cannot be represented by a single character code in the context of the constant.

Executable code

The assembled/compiled and linked code that is loaded into the computer and executed. In a source program, executable code is distinguished from code that declares objects and function prototypes and defines object formats.

Expression

A grouping of one or more constant and variable references, function calls, and relational, logical, and arithmetic operators that form to return a numerical or pointer value.

External data

Data objects that are declared external to any procedure. They are accessible to all procedures within their scope. See also "global data."

F

Field

A single entity of data, usually one item of a data type. Collections of fields form files in a database. A field is also called a "data element."

File

A collection of records of a common format in a database.

File scope

The scope of variables and functions that may be accessed only from within a translation unit. Macros, static functions, and static external variables have file scope.

Firmware

Software encoded into a read-only memory (ROM) integrated circuit.

Floating point number

A number used to represent very large and very small numbers and nonintegral values.

Function

A program procedure that may return a value and may accept one or more arguments. A function consists of a function header and a function body.

Function body

The program statements that constitute the local declarations and executable code of a function definition.

Function header

The first statement in a function definition. It specifies the function's return type, identifier, and parameter list.

G

Global data

External data objects that are declared to be within the scope of the entire program.

Global scope

The scope of variables and functions that are accessible to all translation units in the program.

goto

A statement that abrubtly and unconditionally modifies the execution flow to proceed from a remote labeled statement. The *goto* statement specifies a source code label that matches one attached to an executable source code statement elsewhere in the function.

Graphical user interface (GUI)

A common user interface model that uses the graphics capabilities of the screen to support the "desktop" metaphor. A GUI provides generic menu and dialog box functions. Programs written to run under a GUI tend to have the same visual appearance to the user. Windows 3.1 is the most popular GUI.

H

Header source files

Other source files that a program source file includes when it compiles. Header files typically contain things such as global declarations that independently compiled translation units need to see.

Heap

A large, system-controlled buffer of memory from which the program can dynamically allocate and deallocate smaller memory buffers.

Hexadecimal

Base-16 numerical notation. The digits are 0–9, A–F.

I

Identifier

The name of a variable, macro, structure, or function.

Information hiding

An object-oriented and structured programming technique in which data representations and algorithms are not within the scope of those parts of the program that do not need to access them.

Initializer

An expression specified as a variable's first assigned value when the variable comes into scope.

Input/output redirection

A command line option when you run a program that redirects standard input and output to disk files.

Integer

A whole number; a positive or negative value without decimal places.

Integrated development environment (IDE)

A programming system that integrates a source code editor, language translator (compiler or interpreter), linker, and debugger into one package.

Interactive

An operating mode in which the user communicates with the program by using the keyboard and mouse during the program's execution.

Interpreter

A programming language processor that executes the program by interpreting the source code statements one statement at a time. Interpreters are contrasted with compilers, which compile the source code into linkable object code.

Intrinsic data type

A data type, such as *char*, *int*, *float*, etc., whose format and behavior are known to the compiler. See also "user-defined data type."

Iterate

Execute the statements in a loop. Each iteration is one execution of the loop.

Keyword

A word that is reserved by the C programming language. Typical keywords are *if*, *else*, and *while*.

Label

An identifier followed by a colon that names a program statement. The *goto* statement specifies the label associated with the statement that will execute next.

Library

A file of relocatable object programs. Applications reference external identifiers in the library and link their object code files with the library. The linker pulls from the library the object files that contain the referenced external identifiers.

Linker

A systems program that builds an executable program file from a specified group of relocatable object code files. The relocatable object code files can stand alone, or they can be selected from a library.

Local scope

The scope of automatic and static variables that are declared within a function body or as parameters in the function header.

Local variable

A variable that is defined in a statement block and that is not in the scope of outer statement blocks or other functions.

Loop

A group of program statements that iterate—execute repetitively—while or until a specified condition is true.

lvalue

An expression that can be dereferenced to modify memory. It can exist on the left side of an assignment. See also "rvalue."

M

Macro

A statement that assigns source code meaning to an identifier. A macro may have arguments.

Member

A variable within a structure or union.

Memory

The internal storage medium of the computer. In a PC, semiconductor memory is divided into read-only memory (ROM) and random-access memory (RAM).

Menu

An interactive program's screen display of selections from which the user may choose. Each selection corresponds to an action that the program will take.

Multitasking

An operating system model in which multiple programs run concurrently.

Multiuser

An operating system model in which multiple users share the processor. Each user runs programs independently of the other users. Users can run the same or different programs concurrently.

O

Object code

The machine language code that an assembler or compiler generates from source code. To produce executable code, object code must be linked by the linker program with other object code files and with library object code files.

Octal

Base-8 number system. The digits are 0–7.

Operand

The variables and function calls that an expression uses with operators to produce its value.

Operator

The code token that represents how an expression uses its operands to produce its value.

Operating system

The master control program that operates the computer. It maintains the file system and provides a command interface with the user to execute utility and application programs. See also "DOS."

P

Parameter

The declaration in a function's parameter list of a variable that the function expects to be passed to it. This declaration includes the variable's type and identifier and appears in the function's declaration. See "argument" and "prototype."

Parameter list

The comma-separated, parenthetical list of parameter variable declarations in a function header. It specifies the types and identifiers of all the function's parameters.

Platform

A loosely applied term to mean the operating system or the programming environment. The computer itself, such as the "PC platform" or the "Macintosh platform." The operating environment, such as the "DOS platform" or the "Windows platform." The software development environment of a programming language, such as the "Visual C++ platform" or the "Smalltalk platform."

Pointer

A variable that can contain the address of functions or other variables. The item pointed to can be referenced through the pointer.

Precedence

The property that determines the order in which different operators in an expression are evaluated.

Preemptive multitasking

A multitasking operating system model that does not require handshakes from the running programs. The operating system preempts the running program to allow others to run. Programs are given time slices within which they can run before they are preempted. Programs of higher priority can preempt programs of lower priority at any time.

Preprocessor

A program that reads source code and translates it into source code suitable for the compiler. The preprocessor defines and resolves macros, includes other source code files, and causes specified lines of code to be included or deleted based on conditional expressions.

Program

A collection of computer instructions that execute in a logical sequence to perform a defined task. To write a program.

Program flow control statement

A statement that controls the flow of execution. The *if*, *do*, *while*, *for*, *else*, *break*, *continue*, and *goto* statements are program flow control statements.

Proper programming

A programming model in which procedures have one entry point at the top, one exit point at the bottom, and no endless loops.

Prototype

The declaration of a function's name, return type, and parameter list.

Pulldown menu

A menu that pops down, usually from a menu bar, on top of the screen display. After the user makes a menu selection, the menu pops up to uncover the displays that it obscured.

RAM

Random access memory. Volatile semiconductor memory. Most of the PC's internal memory is RAM.

Random file

A file with fixed-length records that can be accessed in random sequence by addressing the record number.

Real number

A number represented in a program with digits and a decimal point. See also "floating point number."

Real-time

The ability of a program to respond to external events when they happen. The program's execution may not delay its reaction to those events. A spacecraft's guidance system uses real-time processing. Also refers to a program's ability to emulate events within time constraints that match the user's perception of the passage of time. A flight simulator is an example of such a real-time program.

Recursion

The ability of a function to call itself directly or indirectly from functions that it calls.

Reference, pass by

Pass a pointer to the actual argument. The called function acts upon the caller's copy of the argument. See also "value, pass by."

Relocatable object code

Compiled or assembled object code with relative, unresolved memory address references. The references are resolved by the linker program when it builds an executable program from one or more relocatable object files.

Reusable code

Functions that perform utility and general-purpose operations to be used by many unrelated programs.

ROM

Read-only memory. Nonvolatile semiconductor memory. The PC's BIOS is stored in ROM. A program may not change the values written in ROM, and the values persist when power is turned off.

rvalue

An expression that cannot be on the left side of an assignment because it represents a value that might not be taken from a memory location. See also "lvalue."

S

Scope

The range of source code that can access an identifier. An external identifier typically is in scope within the source code file in which the object is declared. In C, the scope extends from the position of the declaration to the end of the file. A global identifier's scope extends to all of the program's source code files. A local identifier is in scope only within the statement block in which it is declared.

Sequential file

A file of fixed- or variable-length records that are accessed in the sequence in which the records occur in the file.

Shareware

A technique for marketing software in which users try the programs first and pay for them only if they want to continue using them.

Side effects

The behavior of a macro that references an argument more than once. If multiple evaluations of an expression can change its meaning or imply unnecessary overhead, the expression is said to have side effects when it is used as an argument to such a macro.

Source code

Assembly or high-level programming language code statements.

Stack

A memory buffer from which the system allocates space for function arguments and automatic variables.

Standard C

The C language as defined by the ANSI X3J11 Committee.

Standard input/output devices

The device files that are usually assigned to the keyboard and screen but that may be redirected to disk files.

Statement

A C language body of code that is terminated with a semicolon.

Statement block

A group of statements that starts with a left brace ({) and ends with a right brace (}).

Storage class

The manner in which a variable is stored in memory, as *auto*, *extern*, *static*, or *register*.

String constant

A null-terminated, variable-length array of characters coded within an expression surrounded by double quotes.

Structure

A record format consisting of one or more objects of multiple data types.

Structured programming

A programming model that uses the three control structures: sequence, selection, and iteration. Structured programming has been extended to include the principles of modular programming as well.

Subscript

An integer value used in an expression to reference an element of an array.

Systems Program

As opposed to "applications program." A program—such as an operating system—that supports the computer system rather than the functional application.

T

Test

The application of a condition to alter the sequence of instruction execution. The *if* and *while* control structures are tests.

Top-down design

Designing a program beginning at the highest level of execution and proceeding downward. The programmer designs the program's entry point and the calls to lower procedures. Each design of a lower procedure decomposes the design into lower and more detailed levels of abstraction until the final design at the lowest level is an expression of the program's algorithms.

Translation unit

The source code and header files that combine to form one independently compiled object module.

Type

The type—*int*, *char*, *float*, etc.—of a variable.

Type qualifier

A qualifying keyword in a variable declaration that specifies whether the variable is *const* or *volatile*.

Typecast

See "cast."

Unary operator

An operator, such as *sizeof*, that has only one operand.

User-defined data type

A data type that the programmer builds by using *struct*, *union*, or *typedef*. See also "intrinsic data types."

User interface

The interactive dialog between the program and the user. In the early days of the PC, user interfaces were invented or contrived by the programmer for each new program. That is why each spreadsheet, word processor, and so on, had its own unique command structure. Users had to learn a different procedure for each program. Contemporary programs are written to run within operating environments, such as Windows, that support a common user interface.

Utility program

A program that performs a utility function in support of the operating environment or the file system. The MS-DOS CHKDSK program is a utility program that tests the integrity of the file system.

Value, pass by

Pass the value of argument. The called function acts upon its own copy of the argument, leaving the caller's copy intact. See also "Reference, pass by."

Variable

An object in memory in which value can be modified by the program at any time.

W

Watchpoint

A debugging procedure in which the debugger watches a memory variable for a specified value or a specified expression for a true condition. When the watchpoint condition is satisfied, the debugger stops the program's execution at the point where the condition became true.

White space

Spaces, newlines, and tab characters in a source code text file.

Index

Installing Quincy 4.1 and the Exercise Programs

To install:

1. Log onto the source diskette drive (a: or b:).
2. Enter this command:

    install c:\qnc

    Where c: is the destination drive and \qnc is the subdirectory.

To run Quincy:

1. Log onto the drive and subdirectory where you installed Quincy.
2. Type **QNC** at the DOS command line prompt.
3. To start the Tutorial, press **Alt+H**, **T**, **U**.